Kashmir Shaivism

And

Modern Science

By

Sham S. Misri

And

Dr. M. L. Babu

Contents

Introduction

It is said, "He who is refused by everybody will find refuge with Shiva."

Shaivism is associated with Shiva. The followers of Shaivam are called "Shaivas," or "Shaivite," It is one of the most widely followed sects of Hinduism. A Shaivite believes that Shiva is All and in all, the creator, preserver, and destroyer. They revere the god Shiva as the Supreme Being.

Shaivism is the oldest living faith in the world. Shiva is our God and Kashmir Shaivism claims to be superior to any other Shiva philosophy. Kashmiri Shaivism does not advocate a life of renunciation. It recommends an active householder's life with daily practice of worship, yoga and meditation. All other gods and goddesses are worshipped as various manifestations of Shiva and Shakhti.

There are several important schools of the Kashmir Shaivism, of which the most elevated belong to the Trika system.

The word "trika" is the Sanskrit for "trinity", suggesting the essential idea that everything in the universe has a threefold nature.

This trinity can be expressed as: Shiva (God), Shakti (His fundamental creative energy) and Anu (the individual, the limited projection of the divinity).

Trika includes several spiritual schools:

1. Krama - in Sanskrit "process", "order", "controlled succession".

2. Kaula (Kula) - in Sanskrit "community", "family", "totality".

3. Spanda - term denoting the Supreme Divine, Creative Vibration.

4. Pratyabhijna - term referring to the direct recognition of the Divine Essence.

These branches of the Shaivite tradition were brilliantly synthesized and unified by the greatest spiritual person of this system, the sage Abhinavgupta.

The most important work he wrote Tantraloka, in verse, unifies all the apparent differences between the Shaivite branches or schools of the Kashmir Shaivism until that moment, offering a coherent and complete vision of the system.

Kashmir Shaivism is a yogic philosophy. Kashmir was a center of learning from ancient times. About 1500 years ago, this advanced spiritual and intellectual culture developed over time, a philosophy of the fundamental nature of the universe and Supreme Consciousness, or Shiva that became known as Kashmir Shaivism.

History

It is very difficult to determine the early history of Shaivism. The Śvetāśvatara Upanishad (400 - 200 B.C.) is the earliest written document describing philosophy of Shaivism.   Theology elevates Rudra to the status of Supreme Being; the Lord who is inspiring yet also has cosmological functions, as does Siva in later traditions.

During the Gupta Dynasty (c. 320 - 500 CE) Puranic religion developed and Shaivism spread rapidly, eventually throughout the subcontinent, spread by the singers and composers of the Puranic narratives.

The worship of Shiva is a Hindu tradition, practiced widely across all of India, Sri Lanka and Nepal. Shaivism has many different schools showing both regional variations and differences in philosophy. Some people believe that artifacts from Mohenjo-Daro, Harappa and other archaeological sites of north-western India and Pakistan indicate that some early form of Shiva worship was practiced in the Indus Valley. These artifacts include lingams and the "Pashupati seal" that point to Shiva worship. The Indus Valley civilization reached its peak around 2500-2000 BC, when trade links with Mesopotamia are known to have existed. The trade was in decline by 1800 BC, and faded away by 1500 BC.

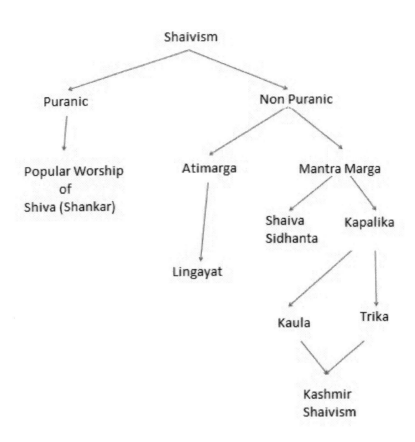

History of Kashmir Shaivism

Disclaimer

The tradition of the Kashmir Shaivism was transmitted from master to disciple centuries in a row, according to the method named "from mouth to ear".

"The symbol of Shiva's cosmic dance unifies mythology, religious art, and modern physics.

In the entire tradition of the Kashmir Shaivism there are present numerous artists who manifested their talents in parallel with the sages and the masters belonging to the Trika school, who had themselves powerful artistic senses.

Thus, the great sage Abhinavgupta composed several poems in the glory of the Lord and wrote almost his entire work in verse, just as the other Shaivite sages.

From Abhinavagupta's point of view, art is a manifestation that is both exterior, and interior in nature, a deeply spiritual manifestation.

Abhinavgupta indicates that the role of art is to awaken a certain inexpressible taste, a sublime feeling, completely and definitely different from all other common human perceptions.

It has a general character, and it is a cosmic perception. On the basis of this intense emotion (anger, joy, fear, amazement, etc.), experienced in a fully aware manner, art determines the passage from individual (ego) to universal.

Kashmir Shaivism appeared in the 9th century in the northern India, which was at the time a small feudal kingdom. The maharajahs were the patrons of the various religions.

The life in the Kashmir valley taught the philosophers a simple, yet detailed path to reach the ultimate purpose of life. In the region of Kashmir, the Shaivite philosophy was kept simple. The Shaivite philosophy did not prescribe any "tortures" for the body or for the brain through painful mortification, and it did not prescribe exterior practices of self-imposed control of the mind, senses and breath, as it is said in other schools of Hindu philosophy. On the other hand, the Kashmir Shaivism recommends a few precise methods of spontaneous meditation, free from any kind of repression and constraint of the mind or of the emotions.

These methods indicate how one can gradually transfer the emotions and instincts through the practice of several meditation and concentration techniques.

The Kashmir Shaivism is the result of deep and profound experiences and meditations practiced by the aspirates that did not have to worry about physical or mental issues.

Therefore, this line of practice usually had to be preceded by other stages of the yoga system.

4th Century A.D.

Kashmir Shaivism has been the most valuable contribution of Kashmir to the Indian culture. This philosophy had basically originated in the trans-Himalayan areas near the Kailasa around the 4th century A.D.

According to the tradition of the Kashmir Shaivism, Shiva established 64 systems, of philosophies, some of them monist, others dualist and few of them monist-dualist. As some of these systems were lost, Shiva asked the sage Durvaasa to revigorate the knowledge.

The sons of Durvaasa, born through the force of the mind were thus designed to transmit the systems as follows: Tryambaks - the monist, Amardaka - the dualist and Shrikantha - the monist-dualist.

Thus, at a certain point, it is said that Tryambaks laid the foundations of the Kashmir Shaivism philosophy and practice. It is also said that Shiva himself felt the need to solve the conflictual interpretations of the sacred writings (agamas) and to cast away the dualist influence on the ancient monist doctrines.

Traymbakaditya, a disciple of the sage Durvaasa, was the first teacher of this school. Sangmaditya, the sixteenth descendant in the line of Tryambaks, settled in Kashmir in the eighth century A.D.

9th Century A.D.

Vasugupta

The first Shaivite works were written in the early ninth century and are attributed to Vasugupta. It is said that the great sage Vasugupta was living on the mountain Mahadeva, near Srinagar. The tradition goes that one night Shiva appeared in a dream and revealed to him the secret place of a great scripture carved on stone. When he woke up, Vasugupta went to that place and found 77 engraved verses carved on a rock, which he then named Shiva Sutra. Then Vasugupta revealed the verses to his disciples and gradually the philosophy spread.

The school of the Kashmir Shaivism or Northern Shaivism Pratyabhijna Darshan, (the doctrine of recognition), Trikasasana (The Trika system of trinity) appeared on this scriptural foundation.

Trika (threefold, triad) refers to the triple consideration of the divine: Shiva, (the masculine principle), Shakti (the feminine principle) and Anu (the individual soul), the possession of three sets of scriptures and of a number of other triads on which this system is based.

The Kashmir Shaivism School originated and developed fully in the valley with the same name, among the beautiful surroundings of this country, as Kashmir is a tranquil and cold area, which gave birth to calm, charming philosophical thinking.

This is why the Kashmir philosophers unlike the philosophers from most of the world, have given up all dogmatic disciplines, and "orthodox" ethics and have pleaded for several effective and pleasant practices in a system they named Shiva yoga (the yoga of the union with Shiva) - a certain type of raja yoga, helped and assisted by the sentiment of a deep, intense love for God.

The life in the Kashmir valley taught the philosophers a simple, yet detailed path to reach the ultimate purpose of life. In the region of Kashmir the Shaivite philosophy was kept simple. The Shaivite philosophy did not prescribe any "tortures" for the body or for the brain through painful mortification, and it did not prescribe exterior practices of self-imposed control of the mind, senses and breath, as it is said in other schools of Hindu philosophy.

On the other hand, the Kashmir Shaivism recommends a few precise methods of spontaneous meditation, free from any kind of repression and constraint of the mind or of the emotions.

Vasugupta had an ambitious agenda. He taught his disciple how to achieve two important goals: to become fully divine and to become fully human. Guru Vasugupta taught them to Kallata and others. Kallata taught them to Kshemaraja who added a commentary, called Vimarshini, to the sutras.

The sutras emphatically declares that man's consciousness in its essential nature, is Atman and the Atman itself is Shiva, the great Lord. Expanding on the Shiva Sutra, Vasugupta composed the Spanda Karika, which describes the limitless power of awareness.

Agama Sastras includes the works considered of divine inspiration, particularly in the Shaiva Agama literature, including the Shiva Sutras a work of capital importance attributed to the sage Vasugupta or to his disciple Kallata (about 850-900).

Bhatta Kallata praises his guru for the blessing of ferrying his boat across the ocean of doubts through his illuminating teachings.

Somananda

He lived at the end of the ninth century, wrote the Vision of Shiva (Shivadrshti). This work develops the principles of Shiva Sutras. The main components of Pratyabhijna Shastra are Shiva Drishti, work of Vasugupta's disciple, Somananda.

Utpaladeva

Utpaladeva was a student of Somananda. The master had taught his student Utpaladeva the philosophy of Kashmir Shaivism. Later on Utpaladeva wrote the Ishwara-Pratyabhijna karika.

After this, and parallel to it have developed other spiritual lines of Kula and Krama.

10th Century A.D.

Abhinavgupta

He was the famous sage-philosopher of Kashmir Shaivism. He lived from the middle of the 10th century into the 11th. He gave Kashmir Shaivism its modern shape. He was one of the greatest and most influential yogis of all time. His contribution to literature has been great. He was the expert master in a field of spirituality.

Abhinavgupta was born in Kashmir to an illustrious family of scholars around 950 C.E. He was brilliant, and so passionate about learning that he hunted out the best teachers of his time. He would advise yoga students thus: "Be like the bee that gathers pollen from many flowers and then makes its own honey. Learn from the greatest masters you can find, then practice and assimilate what you've learned."

He was a creative thinker and had methodically studied aesthetics from his learned guru, Tota Bhatt. Most of the Shiva-gurus have been great lovers of music, drama, dance and poetry. They used them as resource to share the finest aesthetics of Shiva as the source of beauty.

Abhinavgupta is probably the most prominent figure of the Kashmir Shaivism. He wrote almost 40 works including Tantraloka, a text on the Agama Shiva philosophy and ritual. Kashmir Shaivism established as an important philosophical school due to the bright encyclopaedic works written by this great sage.

He was a great scholar and a yogi. At the close of his life he disappeared into a cave near Srinagar to perform strong yogic disciplines. According to legend, twelve hundreds of his students entered the cave with him. They wanted to devote the rest of their lives to meditation in the presence of this great master. He was one of the brilliant and generous spiritual teachers in the history of yoga.

Abhinavgupta explains that the universe doesn't exist apart from Shiva. He says, Shiva is consciousness (chit) which doesn't merely take things without interest, but has the ability to reflect back on itself, to know itself (vimarsha). This self-knowledge is the source of infinite delight (ananda). This bliss in turn is the source of creative activity (Kriya). When Shiva's limitless awareness expands out, the universe comes into existence. And we, as figments of Shiva's imagination, experience ourselves as individual being moving through a world that Shiva's will hold in place. When Shiva withdraws its awareness back into its silent depths, the universe subsides into perfect tranquility.

Kashmir Shaivism: Trika & Its Three Divisions

Kashmir Shaivism has three main divisions corresponding to its three Shastras:

I) The Agama Shastra

II) The Spanda Shastra

III) The Pratyabhijna Shastra

All the three Shastras together, are generally known as Trika Shastra. All those systems of thought which evolved from Shaivagamas and Shaiva Tantras are Shaivism. A Shaiva system means any system based on Shaiva Tantras or Agamas.

Sixty-four systems of the Shaiva cult are mentioned in the Shaiva scriptures of Kashmir which includes the Trika as one of them. Trika is a triad, a group of three divisions of Kashmir Shaivism, Agama, Spanda and Pratyabhijna.

Trika deals with the triple principle of, Shiva, Shakti and Anu; or Pati, Pasha and Pashu; or Nara, Shakti and Shiva; or Para, Apara and Parapara.

Besides this, the three systems, Bheda (dualism), Abheda (non-dualism) and Bheda- bheda (dualism-cum-non-dualism) are also included in Trika philosophy.

Tantraloka – It is a Compendium of Trika Shastra:

Tantraloka, by Abhinavgupta, includes the contents of all the three branches of Kashmir Shaivism (Trika-Shastra), viz. Agama, Spanda and Pratyabhijna in a summarized form. The Tantraloka is a most voluminous work of Abhinavgupta, composed in verse, and forms an encyclopedia of the Trika Shastra.

Philosophical aspect of Trika-Shastra

Trika Shastra the three divisions of Kashmir Shaivism, represents, in its philosophical context, a concept of positivism in a theistic outlook.

According to them, Shiva, the Ultimate Reality, is the creative cause: 'essence and identity' (Self) of everything. He abounds in bliss and consciousness and is gifted with sovereignty of will. He knows everything, and is all powerful. He is everything and yet beyond everything. Time, form and space do not limit him, for; He is above all mutation and change. 'Pashu' (a living being) being the fragment of the inter-related whole is no other than Shiva Himself, but is in a state of limitation and self-forgetfulness.

The Agama Shastra of Kashmir includes rigid philosophy. Some of them are mostly religious. Some of them give the basics of Kashmir Shaivism. They teach certain methods, and mystical practices (upayas) for achieving lower and higher Siddhi (supernatural powers) and the glories of life.

Shaivism, the Trika, focuses on three main universal issues. First, it inquires into the nature of consciousness, the nature and oneness of reality and of God.

Next it talks about contraction, the material world, that which separates us from Consciousness, and finally it sets forth the means of Sadhana, the method that liberates us from suffering and returns us to oneness.

If there were only God, and no tension, then we would be in constant bliss. But, life is full of tension and struggle. As soon as Consciousness becomes fine there is suffering. If we are Shiva, we are Shiva in prison. Shiva became intoxicated with His creation and managed to forget His true nature.

The third aspect of the Trika is Sadhana, yogic practice. The great Shaivite yogis developed a methodology to get rid of our metaphysical bondage. Sadhana is the path back to our original condition, back to Shiva. It culminates in Self-realization. Sadhana, the method liberates us from suffering and returns us to oneness. If there were only God, and no tension, then we would be generous in constant bliss. But life is full of tension and struggle. We may feel that we lack something that would improve our situation, or we may feel we have lost something that was necessary. Both conditions create conflict, and contraction. As soon as consciousness becomes contracted there is suffering.

I. Agama Shastra (Sadhana-Shastra)

It is believed to be of divine origin. Shiva Sutras are said to be the most important part of the Agama Shastra.

Agama-Shastra is mostly Sadhana-Shastra; i. e., it mainly deals with ritualistic and mystic practices. Usually, every Agama consists of four sections or Kandas

a) Vidya or Jnana Kanda

(Section dealing with secret knowledge),

b) Yoga Kanda

(Section dealing with Yoga discipline, processes of concentration and breathing exercises-pranayama),

c) Kriya Kanda

(Section dealing with action, viz, ritualistic performances)

d) Carya Kanda

(Section deals with forms of worship)

e) Tantric Shakhti

From the valley of Kashmir in northern India, the principles of Shaivism were first written down in the ninth century. Shaivism represents a basic view on the Universe. It allows us to understand the true nature of Agama's Tantric practice.

In Tantric, the term Shakti defines an unbelievable complex aspect of the universe. The Tantrics assert that in order to define Shakti one has to know 'Her'. According to the tantric view of Shakti, She has countless ways of manifesting herself.

She is the famous energy Kundalini or the snake coiled at the base of the spine, immense energy that yogis awaken and think with appeal, charm and fear equally, totally charmed by it. The snake is merely a symbol of the spiritual path, not the path itself.

In the case of people, this snake is envisaged as coiled three times and a half at the base of the sacrum, in the force center Muladhara Chakra. Kundalini represents Shakti's force in the microcosm of the human being.

One of the goals of the Tantric practitioner is to awaken this "snake of feminine energy" and to make it ascend along the spine through the six chakras, to the crown of the head, to be united with the pure consciousness residing there. When this occurs, the person experiments the state of Samadhi - divine ecstasy.

"O", Mother Kundalini! Coiled in the center of Muladhara, you awaken the universe to the existence, when you rise in a wreath of flames up to Sahasraras where you are united with Siva." (Tantrasara)

There is a Hindu myth about how Shakti first appeared. The legend says that a monstrous demon, Mahisha, was threatening the foundation of the universe itself, and the existence of all gods. Brahma and all famous people and gods called Shiva and Vishnu for help. Enraged, the gods emitted their energies as a fire coming out from their mouth. These different divine flames unified into a one as a burning cloud, and finally took the shape of a goddess with eighteen arms. This goddess, Shakti was the one who succeeded in defeating the demon and at the same time saving the universe.

It seems that the gods had to somehow restore their energies to the Primitive Force, the Source from which everything emerged in the very beginning. Shakti represents the force of transformation and regeneration, an extraordinary growing force that may lead to ecstasy, in tantric opinion.

Besides, Shakti represents the pure force of orgasm, the thrill of sexual pleasures amplified through the profound fusion between the two lovers. She is the divine game of love itself. She is also called "Lalita" or "Lila", both meaning "the one who plays."

Tantra says: "everything that we see through the eyes is definable, but not 'Her' who is the Mother", and "she is indescribable and beyond perception/conception; having a form, she is nonetheless formless."

f) Maya

The tantrics have distinguished two aspects in which she becomes manifested: static and dynamic. Shakti is Maya, (illusion) who appears as the unique world and hides the Absolute Consciousness from the ignorant.

In her supreme form, Shakti is identified with Mahadevi or Mahamaya, the Great Goddess, the power who creates and destroys, often represented as the mysterious uterus from which everything emerged and in which everything dissolves.

In the tantric cosmology, the whole universe is considered to have emerged and sustained by two forces, opposed in term of polarity: Shiva (masculine) and Shakti (feminine). She is the colossal force, who supports the biologic, psychic, affective and mental processes of the human being.

In Kashmir Shaivism this phenomenal world (Shakti) is real and it exists and has its bearing in consciousness (chit). In contrast Advaita holds that this phenomenal world is illusion (Maya).

Divine Couple

In Tantra Shakti, "the cosmic feminine force", is raised to the position of Divine Mother who sustains the Universe and all the beings, the multiple manifestation of gods. Women got an essential role in religion and spiritual philosophy for the first time in Tantric practice. Only in Tantra the female principle has got a real role, just as important as the male one. Tantra goes further and presents the Divine Being as a glorious perfect and harmonious combination of feminine and masculine. The Divine couple is presented as the Shiva - Shakti couple in ecstatic union.

In Tantra the woman and the man are complementary and equal in chances of discovering the ultimate reality. By unifying the man and the woman, by love they look different and beautiful; they become the divine couple

Shiva - Shakti. Thus they can complete one another at all levels of being, creating a Glorious healthy women.

Tantra gives an example by comparing the couple Shiva and Shakti with a seed of grain. Such a seed is made up of two halves so closely linked that they seem one, and one single cover, covers them. Symbolically, the two halves represent Shiva and Shakti, the cover represents Maya (the cosmic illusion). When the cover is on, the two halves are separated, but the cover goes off, when the seed is about to germinate, unifying thus the two halves in one.

From very remote times, Brahmins of Kashmir had been performing Vedic rituals which were predominantly vaisnavite in character. The worship of Shiva and Shakti also had become very popular in this land right from the prehistoric ages. There are many very old shrines of Siva in Kashmir.

g) Karma

Karma school is an integral part of Kashmir Shaivism. It is an independent system both philosophically and historically. Karma is significant as a synthesis of Tantra traditions based on the monistic Savism. Karma is merely a law of cause and effect and is also dependent on the will of a personal supreme God. The term karma means 'progression', 'gradation' or 'succession' respectively meaning 'spiritual progression or 'gradual refinement of the mental processes'(vikalpa), or 'successive unfoldment taking place at the ultimate level', in the Supreme Consciousness (chit).

"God does not make one suffer for no reason nor does He make one happy for no reason. God is very fair and gives exactly what one deserves."

Karma is not punishment or revenge but simply an extended expression or consequence of natural acts. Karma means "deed" or "act". More broadly, the universal principle of cause and effect, action and reaction that governs all life is due to karma.

Karma is not fate, for, humans act with free will creating their own destiny. According to the Vedas, if one sows goodness, one will reap goodness; if one sows evil, one will reap evil. Karma refers to the totality of our actions and their related reactions in this and previous lives, all of which determines our future. The conquest of karma lies in intelligent action and dispassionate response.

The most distinctive feature of Karma is its monistic-dualistic (bhedābhedopāya) discipline in the stages prior to spiritual realization. Even if Kashmir Shaivism is monism, there is still a place for dualistic aspect on the spiritual path. So it is said that in practice Karma employs the dualistic-cum-nondualistic methods. Karma aims at forming a synthesis of enjoyment (bhoga) and illumination (mokṣa).

h) Aham

Aham, a concept of Kashmir Shaivism, is defined as the supreme heart (hṛdayam), transcendent Self, supreme I awareness or infinite consciousness. The space of Aham is where kechari mudra (free movement in the space of the heart) is realised. Kechari mudra is considered the supreme state of spiritual evolution.

When Siva wants to create, the first step is said to be the creation of an interior space (the space of his heart) - a matrix of energies that will be the substrate of the new world. This place is called Aham which means "I" in

Sanskrit. Thus the absolute first creates the divine person, Aham, and from this divine person will appear the manifestation itself.

Aham is identical to mātṛkā (the wheel of phonematic energies), essential nature of all categories from Pṛithvī tattva (earth) to Sadāśiva tattvas,. Aham is the final resting place, dwelling place, abode of all beings, receptacle of the world.

In Aham, the supreme (para) aspect of Sakti is realized. Aham is the Sakti of Siva or in other words, the expansion of Siva. Another way of describing Aham is as the union of Siva and Sakti.

Aham is formed of A+HA+M, a triad of Shiva (A), Sakti (HA) and bindu (M). M is the final point, union of Śiva and Sakti, where they dissolve into Paramaśiva. The triangle of A+HA+M is the essence of the Trika system. A+HA+M form the sṛṣṭi bīja (seed of emission), a mantra that is identical to the energy of expansion and creation.

Aham can also be defined as: A = abedha (non-differentiation), HA = bheda (differentiation) and M = bhedābheda (differentiation cum non-differentiation).

Maha, the mirror image of Aham

On the other hand, MAHA, mirror image of AHAM, is formed of MA+HA+A, and represents the saṃhara bīja (seed of reabsorption) - the mantra that is identical to the process of spiritual evolution, or in other words reabsorption of the manifestation back into the absolute. In MAHA, Sakti (HA) enters bindu (M) (the limited being) and reunites it with the Supreme (A).

Aham, the Heart of Siva

Aham is the concept of supreme reality as heart. It is considered to be a non-dual interior space of Siva, support for the entire manifestation, supreme mantra and identical to Sakti.

i) Kapalikas

It is a strong monistic interpretation of Bhairava Tantras (Kauls Tantras) written by Kapalikas. Kashmir Shaivism (Kapalikas Shaivism):

Kashmir Saivism, a householder religion, was based on a strong monistic interpretation of the Bhairava Tantras (and its subcategory the Kaula Tantras), which were tantras written by the Kapalikas. Sacred ash came to be used as a sign of Shaivism. Devotees of Shiva wear it as a sectarian mark on their foreheads and other parts of their bodies with reverence. The Sanskrit words bhasma and vibhuti can both be translated as "sacred ash".

Kaula

It is said: "The mind is seen as a krama family of agents (Kula), which understands spontaneously the true Self (Pratyabhijna), with a creative power that can make regular movement or sounds. Such movements or sounds in a regular pattern are perceived as pulsatory (spanda)". Although domesticated into a householder tradition, Kashmir Shaivism recommended a *secret* performance of Kaula practices in keeping with its heritage. This was to be done in seclusion from public eyes, therefore allowing one to maintain the appearance of a typical householder.

It is important to distinguish Kashmir Shaivism from Advaita Vedanta of Adi Shankara as both are undualistic which give privacy to universal consciousness (Chit or Brahman). The goal of Kashmir shaivism is to merge in

Shiva, universal consciousness In Advaita this universe is MAYA but in Shaivism this universe is real.

"Let Shiva who is myself, let Siva do pranam to his real nature – to universal Shiva, by his own Shakhti, for removing the bondage and limitation, which is Shiva."

Here, Shiva, bows to himself, for the removal of obstacles, which are also Shiva, through his own energy (Shakhti) which is one with Shiva, and in the end He resides in the state of universal Shiva. That is the state of Para (Supreme) Bhairava.

Trika

Trika philosophy teaches that this world is nothing but the blissful energy of the all-pervading consciousness of Lord Shiva.

In Trika Shaivism, although the word Trika means three, everything is found in state of oneness. From the Trika point of view there is not the slightest difference between individual soul and lord Shiva, it is just a play, a drama of his own nature

Shiva is infinite consciousness, is both imminent and transcendent and is the object reality underlying the universe from which everything ensues and into which everything dissolves.

Shakhti is the dynamic energy of Shiva. She has an infinitely of aspects such as chit Shakhti (power of intelligence), ananda Shakhti (Power of freedom), Iccha Shakhti (Power of will), Jana Shakhti (Power of knowledge), Kriya Shakhti (The power creative action). This objective world is expansion of Shakhti. Since Shiva is ultimate reality, Shakhti should not be mistaken as something different from Him. Shakhti is an indistinguishable aspect of Shiva, performing a specific set of tasks, with no distinction of her own. The duality is an illusion created by our own ignorance and limitations.

The World which we live in is a projection of Shiva's dynamism. If God is real, everything emanating from it must be real. By his free will Shiva manifests the objective reality within himself, using himself as the quality of nature, the source (Tattvas) and substratum.

So this world is only a reflection within himself without independent existence of its own. Thus according to Kashmir Shaivism, Siva and his creation are both real and inseparable. He creates this world through his dynamic for pure joy of rediscovering Himself through his individual selves. Using his free will he hides himself or conceals his God consciousness in his limited selves, in order to rediscover himself.

According to Kashmir Shaivism there is no difference Shiva and Jiva.

Through his dynamic Shakhti he creates temporary ignorance in' jivas' and subjects them to treat impurities of anava, Karma, Maya, because of which they believe themselves to be finite and separate and subject themselves to the laws of karma. The purpose of each jiva is, therefore, to recognize its own nature and experience its original Shiva consciousness.

According to Kashmir Shaivism, there are three paths (upayas), stages of attaining the supreme consciousness or Shiva consciousness. They are:

a) Sambavopa- In this jiva surrenders oneself completely to lord and waits for his grace.

b) Shaktopaya- In this liberation occurs through Shakhti. In this Jiva has a one point concentration, or he awakens his kundalini. No role of Mantras, prayers, in this method. He will transcend his impurities and experience his consciousness.

c) Anavopaya- In this liberation is through personal effort. Recitation of Mantras, prayers, meditation. Breathing exercises are included this.

There is also a fourth path, anupaya, "without means", which consists in a mature recognition of the Self. On this path, nothing needs to be done, attained, or fulfilled, except for remaining in one's own being, which is Shiva.

*Trika means Trinity of Nara Shakhti, and Shiva as given in Tantras.

Nara-means individual.

Shakhti- Universal energy.

Shiva- Transcendental Energy. (Mystical life). This transcendental energy is three fold.

1) Para- is subjective energy and supreme.

2) Para para- is intermediate. It is reasoning energy.

3) Apara energy- It is inferior and is objective energy. Human has this energy.

II. Spanda Shastra: (Energy) Vibrations.

Spanda-Shastra founded by Bhatta Kallata (9th century). The original text belonging to this Shastra and the literature developed on it have been (missing text). Spanda describes the power of consciousness which infuses life into the physical senses. Spanda Karikas (verses) are 51 in number. They are the fundamental principles of Shaivism; In fact, the Spanda system owes its origin to the Shiva Sutras and concerns itself with their clarification and popularization.

The basic idea underlying the Spanda-Shastra is that Shiva's Spanda (energy) out of its own self. According to this doctrine, the world is a play of energy force or vibration, which appears to be in conformity with the modern science. It is not an illusion, the result of error in awareness. Discovery of modern physics that matter is only waves of various lengths, without their being any essentially solid, hard stuff is really a re- discovery of what the Trika Shastra conceived centuries ago as the "Spanda".

Through modern physics, we have grown accustomed to thinking of physical reality as waves of energy--as the matter-energy continuum. Tantric Shaivism presents the full matrix of energy pulsation of which physical reality is only a part. From the relatively superficial perceptions of the senses to the progressively subtle forms of inner awareness, a unified spectrum of spanda leads inward until the most delicate and powerful tendrils of individuality merge with the infinitely rapid vibration of the ultimate consciousness.

III.   Praty abhijna Shastra: (Recognition)

Somananda was the founder of the Pratyabhijna School. Pratyabhijna system is the philosophical school of the Kashmir Shaivas. Abhinavgupta great teacher of Kashmir Shaivism) gets the credit of being the teacher of Pratyabhijna system. Somananda flourished in the later part of the ninth century A. D., Utpaladeva in the first part of the tenth century and Abhinavgupta in the last part of the tenth and the first part of the eleventh century.

Pratyabhijna has been admitted to be a taraka Shastra (a system of logic and philosophy).

Pratyabhijna Philosophical school of Kashmir Shaivism is very old. Though its introduction in Kashmir is shrouded in mystery, it was prevalent there long before the time of Asoka (273-232 B. C.). Eighth and ninth centuries of the Christian era seem to have witnessed a religious upheaval in Kashmir. This followed a philosophic new beginning in the valley. Kashmir was then a meeting ground of the various philosophical currents.

Pratyabhijna Shastra emerged in the valley among the followers of Shaiva cult. It was they who gathered some thoughts from the meetings of the then prevailing schools of Buddhists, the Shaivas and Shakti, and the Yoga system, that a monistic school of philosophy, known as Pratyabhijna came into being. The Kashmir Shaiva, incorporated in it most of the ideas of various doctrines and added some technique of their own derived from the Shaivagamas, which distinguish the system from the other systems.

Somananda revolted against the prevailing schools of thought, including certain sections of Shaivas themselves. He criticized the various schools of Buddhism, the Jainism, and the monistic Vedanta. It appears that Somananda was against the traditional ideas about the divinity, the meaning and purpose of life, the human activities and behaviors on earth, the real significance of 'Moksha' (salvation or liberation) and the like. This new school came later to be known as 'Pratyabhijna School' (the doctrine of Recognition), composed by Somananda's disciple Utpaladeva.

'Pratyabhijna' is recognition. It comprehends the sense of awareness, consciousness, realization, 'knowledge in practice' or practical use of knowledge. Pratyabhijna school thinks that man is ignorant and unaware of the very nature of one's own Self (Shiva-Atman), viz. his inner being. The man is ignorant about great sense within him, and its power of 'Iccha' (Will), 'Jnana' (knowledge, Thought) and 'Kriya' (Action), viz., man's abilities with which he is gifted by fate.

The school believes that the powers or abilities, with which man is born in this world, comprise his supreme (divine) inheritance. It is only then, when he becomes aware of his divine inheritance, that he can make the best use of it in making his life successful.

Pratyabhijna is, in its essence, a deep and systematic study of man as small, and the world he lives in as big.

The Pratyabhijna is directed to removing the veil of ignorance from us and turning our attention towards the deeper faculties within us. Pratyabhijna says (hints) with emphasis that knowledge put into action or practice is really meaningful.

Pratyabhijna is one of the greatest humanistic movements of Kashmir, which might well be called the 'Philosophy of Humanism'. It is a wonderful synthesis of nearly all earlier systems of India's philosophic thinking, and is completely free from 'negativism' and escapism' of certain schools of Vedanta's.

It is most realistic in its attitude to life. Pratyabhijna lays emphasis on human values and basic virtues.

According to Pratyabhijna, human beings are by nature divine. They are the sparks of the divine, children of God. The whole mankind forms one family. It is by self-discipline (culture) and clean moral life that man can unveil the divine qualities in his personality. Love of God in this school means love of human beings. He, who loves God, loves everybody and looks on all men as equals. Love of God is to be translated into service of one's fellow – men.

Gentleness, righteousness, sympathy, friendliness and honest dealings with one another are qualities or virtues necessary for good life. Pratyabhijna promotes the values of peace and freedom and human dignity beneficial to the common man.

These values are stated in terms like 'sarva-shivata' (which signifies that the personality of every human individual is divine or sacred), 'sarva-samata' (meaning that all men are born equal) 'sarva - svatantrya' (i.e. all men are born free) and so on. Thus the doctrine lays emphasis on 'liberty, equality and fraternity' which is the famous motto of 'the civilized world today. Above all, Pratyabhijna directs man to working for peace and tranquility of the world (Vishva-

Shanti). Following the truth is conducive to the good and benefit of the whole humanity. The Pratyabhijna is said to be another way of realization, a way of mere knowledge (awareness) and reasoning (taraka).

12th Century A.D.

Kshemaraja

Kshemaraja was Abhinavagupta's closest disciple and a student. Kshemaraja was a commentator, not one of the founding sages or great innovators. He wrote many treatises in the 12th century. In his highly praised commentary on Shiva-Sutra, Kshemaraja informs that guru is one who teaches Reality or Truth. He reveals the power of mantra to his pupils. The original Shaivite texts, the 'Shiva Sutras' and 'Spanda Karikas are hard to categorize. They are mysterious and wonderful! That is one reason why Kshemaraja's text is helpful, well-structured and logical.

The sage Kshemaraja says, 'in this world, nothing exists which is outside the range of Consciousness'.

Consciousness is the supreme light by which everything else shines; it holds everything within itself.

In Tantra, guru is described as one who fully knows the essentials of thought (Kashmir Shaivism). The guru throws light on the power of Mantras. In Tantra, guru is said to have power of grace. If pleased with his disciple, guru reveals to him all the hidden truth about Shiva's manifestation of the universe.

Guru is a liberator, up lifter and path finder of the aspirants who want to pursue the path of spiritual quest. He is a crutch to those who are lacking in Shiva consciousness. Guru is a vital link between a seeker and his ultimate destination.

The centre of Kashmir Shaivism was at Srinagar in Kashmir and the Amarnath cave near Srinagar, where there is a naturally occurring Shiva linga or symbol of the God, is a centre of pilgrimage for many Shaivas.

14th Century A.D.

The middle of the 14th century was a period of religious and moral activity and excitement in Kashmir Valley. Buddhism had practically disappeared from the Valley. Most of the Buddhist saints finding the Valley unfriendly had left for Ladakh and Tibet. The peaceful period and reign of Avantivarman (855-83 A.D.) was responsible for the rigidness of the main religion Shaivism. It had complicated and difficult rituals. Shaivism had dominated all social and cultural 'natural' (Svayambhu) images - rocks, or ice formations, or springs. Sanskrit became the domain of the learned few. The common man was wholly different from the 'Language of the Gods'.

It is believed that phonetic distortion and decay in Sanskrit gave rise to Apabhramsha followed later by Prakrit. Kashmiri emerged as a language towards the close of the 14th Century. Kashmiri language assumed some form in its original base of Sanskrit. Till then Shaivism had expressed itself as the doctrine of Self recognition. The doctrine had made an appeal with its love and devotion. Shaivism was regarded as the main faith. Great intellects like Abhinavgupta, Utpaladeva, Kshemendra and other saints, seers and scholars had enriched this thought and culture with their contributions. As a belief of peaceful thought Shaivism inspired love and affection in human hearts. It discarded all the painful and tortuous methods of seeking God. This soothing faith found a wide appeal across the Himalayan frontiers into Tibet, China, Kabul, and Kandahar.

Shiva Ratri is the celebration of Lord Shiva's cosmic play. It is a day of self-realization for getting the perfect glimpse of Lord Shiva. It suggests us to be in tune with the Shiva-consciousness.

Kashmiri Hindus observe the Maha Shivratri with great pomp and show. They have associated it with the belief and tradition of the union of Siva and Shakti. Many mythological stories are connected with the celebration of the Maha Shivratri popularly known in Kashmir as Herat. We have a belief that Amarnath cave or Ma Shivratri is the impact of Saivism in Kashmir. It is for this that Kashmir enjoys a special position in the globe for giving a dynamic philosophy of day to day living. The Shakti worship that we see in every corner of Kashmir and the impact of Tantra fold prevalent in Kashmir point to the fact that Saivism had deep roots in Kashmir.

Kashmir is one of the Shakti pithas among fifty pithas mentioned in Lalita Sahasranama. Dr. Radhakrishnan has very truly said that spiritual life was the true genius of India. Those who made the greatest appeal to the Indian mind were not the military conquerors, not the rich merchants or the great diplomats but the holy sages, the Rishis who embodied spirituality at its finest and purest. The great sages and seers or the holy men had the vision to realize the truth according to the need and requirement of the time.

Lalleshwari (1320-1392)

Lalleshwari or Lal Ded was the first Kashmiri saint poetess who expressed the Shaiva philosophy in a charming poetic style in the modern Kashmiri language. She was followed in the tradition by many mystic poets, both Hindus and

Muslims. She talked this philosophy to the masses in Kashmiri and not in Sanskrit. She denounced rituals, narrow-mindedness, fanaticism and reducing the distinction of caste. She has also been one of the greatest supporters of the Kashmir Shaivism commonly known as Trika-philosophy.

The philosophy teaches that the universe is the expression of the Lord Himself and the Lord is to be understood in the very look of the universe. Kashmir Shaivism holds no distinction on the basis of caste, creed or color. Every individual has the capacity to approach the Lord for his or her personal enlightenment. She has given out the philosophy very beautifully in her own style of a master artist in her various poetic compositions.

Gagane paethe bootal shiv yaeli dyeothum, ravas labem na rozan shaai

Sirye kay prabhave shivmaiy zonum, zal gav thalas saet meelith kyah.

Lalleshwari, in one of her personal experiences says that she has experienced the whole universe as a picture of Lord Shiva. It extended from the highest skies to the deepest parts of the earth. It had such a huge form that there seemed no place for the Sun to show its face. Only a few sunbeams that fell on the earth showed a wonderful scene of water and land mingled into one. She was thus able to experience the reality of the vast appearance of her Lord. The description of Shiva in these lines suggests the essential spirit of Kashmir Shaivism (Shunya) that the universe as a whole is the manifestation of Parma Shiva or Shaiva Darshan.

Lall boe looses chaaran te gaaran, hal maey kormas rasnay shati

Wuchun hyotmas te taer wuchmas baran, mae te kal ganaye te zogmas tatey

Lalleshwari describes the abode of her Lord Shiva and the approach of the seeker towards it. She says she had a tough experience in her search of the Lord's house. After getting completely exhausted by visiting places and asking hundreds of people she reaches her destination. Being satisfied she seeks admittance there. To her disappointment she finds all the entries closed for her. She persists and continues with her devotion. Just there and then the doors open for her. She achieves her soul's content by meeting her Lord.

Lall boe draayas shiv gaarnay, wuchum shiv te shakti akey shay

Shakti wuchum paeth sahasraras, maaraan gayas tamey graye

Boe paer shivas te shive sendis garas, boe lall maras te mae kare kyah

Once, Lalleshwari set out in search of her Lord Shiva. She saw Lord Shiva and His royal companion Shakti, a single body with Shakti seated graciously on the head of Shiva. Shakti was seated above the matted coils of His hair. Lall was excited to experience this celestial show that she begins dancing with joy. The seat of Shakti on the head of Lord Shiva indicated the role of the Lord as a preserver of the universe which is the essence of Kashmir Shaiva concept. Lalleshwari was so pleased upon her success that she made a wish of sacrificing her worldly existence at the divine altar as she had all her wishes fulfilled.

Lalla Ded's Vaakhs had intense spiritual abilities which were tapped for final result by her guru, Sidda Srikanth. He was a Shaiva thought and Shaiva Yoga. He was the family guru of Lalla Ded. He had nonstop sessions of debates and discourses with her. This was to sharpen her vision and clarity on issues relevant to the Shaiva thought.

To Lalla Ded, her guru, Sidda Srikanth, was a Parameshwar. He relieved her doubts and misgivings about things not belonging to physical world. What Srikanth, her Guru did with Lalla Ded through Mantra was to direct her mind (chitta) to consciousness of Shiva. Lalla Ded had absolute trust and faith in the word of Shiva-guru. His mantra, and the mind under the control of Shiva consciousness, was the gateway to her final bliss.

About Shunya (Nothingness)

Lal Ded was a great Yogi, a true Shaiva. In her wanderings, through the space she observed big black holes and deep fissures. She cautions all the spiritual saints daring to undertake such an adventure, to travel through the space that they must avoid dangerous routes and move ahead with care. The black holes are objects in the space, which are so dense and gravitationally strong that neither matter nor light can escape them. However, energy is released, as matter plunges into the hole's deep gravity well.

Loob maarun sahaz vyatsaarun, Dro'g zaanun kalpan traav;

Nishi chuy tay duur mo gaarun, Shuunyas shuunyaah miilith gav.

In the above vakh she says: "Realization is rare indeed; seek not afar; it is near, by you. First slay Desire, and then still the mind, giving up vain imaginings; then meditate on the Self within, And lo! The void merges in the Void. Lalleshwari had attained the highest goals of spirituality. She says that concentration on the Lord's name and meditating on one's real self is the key to get rid of the worldly desire. She had a clear imagination that achieving the status of being one with the Lord was not so hard for everyone who wanted to reach there. The main hurdle in the achievement of spiritual goals is one's own incapacity. Lalleshwari has a clear message for a simple devotee ---- your Lord is nearer to you than everything else! Never imagine Him to be far from away! Just keep under control the fiery body emotions. There is no need to seek Him anywhere else. He is there inside your loving heart. The individual soul is an essential part of the supreme. Once it achieves the essential realization of self, it takes a swift flight to meet the Lord and become one with Him. *Atma* becomes one with *Paramatma*. Shunya merges with the absolute. Human being loses its personal identity and becomes one with the Lord. All duality between the ordinary soul and the supreme soul is finished. Lalleshwari had attained this experience and there was nothing further unattainable for her.

"Shuniya" or a "zero point" is where the mind become still and you become the observer. This way you are not the ripple of the waves, but stillness in the depths of the ocean. Shuniya is a deep, meditative state of consciousness where the 'separate' self-identity softens into stillness. This state of being is so pure and clear that it is often referred to as a state of 'zero'. In Shuniya, the greater aspect of 'Self', or the 'higher self', is available and the experience of oneness is realized. The characteristics of Shuniya are inbuilt. The features of shuniya are graceful, soulful, neutral, sensual,

accepting, and allowing. There is no judgment, expectation, opinion, pushing, or intellectualism. It is a pure form of love. In this state of consciousness, the Infinite is in charge and what happens is limitless.

The Masters of Kundalini Yoga, say that the highest state of consciousness is called 'Shuniya', where the ego is brought to complete stillness. A power exists there. We do not hassle or try to act. With folded hands of devotion, Infinity acts for us. In that state of "zero," if we can focus our mental projection on a clear intention, which acknowledges our higher self and the Creator within us, it will be so.

Shuniya, nothing, or no-thing. There is no miracle. The mind is infinite when it concentrates the magnetic energy of the psyche. There are only two things: energy and matter. Any composition, permutation of any energy into matter and matter into energy, can be caused by a disciplined mental concentration. That mental concentration is in you, it is not outside.

Gurus precheome sassi latey, Yas nu kenh vanan tas kyah naav.

Pritschaan pritschaan thachis tu loosis,Kenh nas nishi kyaahtaam draav.

In the above vaakh, Lalla says I requested my spiritual guide, a thousand times, with consciousness: "He that is nameless, how that nameless is named?" Since the curiosity to know is a worship of higher order, it implies a belief in the existence of higher power, without which there could be no worship. It was by gradual process of thought that Lal Ded wanted to become conscious of a new force, for establishing the identity of the Lord. As her soul was in anguish she asked and asked till she became tired, mute and silent. *Lo! The nameless non-existent and invisible became the source of her realization.* This is the beginning of her awakening in spiritual bliss that paved way to enter into the realm of ecstasy, and, that resulted in the realization of *'something evolved out of nothing.'* It was all puzzling but great and wonderful. The Guru directed her in seeing that *Nameless within self.*

The vakh clearly state that when Lal Ded asked her master (Guru) a thousand times what the name of the nameless was and when she had exhausted enquiring repeatedly, she suddenly got awakened to the truth of her enquiry. The truth that was revealed to her was that the ultimate goal of man was only to be one with the universal void (Shunya). The truest truth of the universal Lord is His nothingness. The truth of the total realization of man is getting lost in this sea of nothingness and becoming an indivisible part of the whole.

Again, in another vakh:

Shunyuk maidaan kodum paanas, Mye lalli, roozum na bodh na hosh;

Vezuyi sapnis paanay paanas, Adu kami hilli pholli lalli pamposh!

Here Lalla says: "I travelled far beyond in the space, leaving behind me reason and sense. Then, came upon the secret of the Self; All on a sudden, I experienced a feeling of strange delight. I suddenly lost the entire intelligence, in the bliss of ecstasy. I started realizing my own true spirit rising to the heights of spiritual kindness."

Lalla says: "I travelled alone extensively the higher reaches of my Lord's influence. The sights and scenes were so enchanting that I lost my conscience. But soon I was awakened to the delicate secrets of my inner self. Thus I Lalla with such a humble background was escorted into the crowning glory of celestial emancipation."

Shuniya is a broader concept of the Supreme Lord. It is not anyway comparable to nothingness in its ordinary sense, because, it holds in its purview the whole cosmos as an influence of the Lord. Lalleshwari was a highly awakened soul who had achieved all the goals of divinity. In the ecstasy of her achievement she says she toured the extensive fields of *Shuniya*, the Lord's influence during her celestial journey so much so that she lost all the consciousness of her body sensations but soon upon gaining the awakening of her real self she gained the greatest satisfaction. The achievement is beautifully compared by Lalleshwari to the lovely blossom of a lotus field on the muddy surface of wet lowland which indicates her down to earth background and her subsequent achievement high up into the skies.

Shuniya is not some fancy mysterious yogic term. Through meditation, we can train our minds to respond with a steady consciousness instead of reacting from fluctuating emotions. Through meditation we can reach that still point where we merge with the Infinite and create our own extensive reality. Miracles are developed in the soil of Shuniya.

19th-20th Century

The Revival of Kashmir Shaivism

Kashmir Shaivism went underground for a number of centuries. While there may have been yogis and practitioners quietly following the teachings, there were no major writers or publications after perhaps the 14th century.

Krishna Joo Razdan (1850- 1926)

Pandit Krishna Joo Razdan was born in 1850 at Vanpoh, Distt.Annantnag, Jammu and Kashmir, India. He was a devotee of Shiva. He praised Lord Shiva in all his forms. His work and mystic poems give clear idea about his personality and about his inner consciousness of soul.

'Achhe Posh Gav Lachhi Novuy Heth' is a great devotional lyric of Pt. Krishna Joo Razdan. Here the poet shows deep devotion for Lord Shiva and his Divine Consort, Shakti. The chief mood objectified is devotional ecstasy. This devotional literary work narrates the story of Shiva's union with Shakti.

For Razdan Sahib, Sad Guru is none other than Lord Shiva himself. He longs for the realization of Shiva amidst the illusory cosmos. Through the exercise of self control, he desires liberation from the shackles of lust, wrath, greed, pride and possessiveness. He attained Shiva hood through intense Sadhana, taught by Kashmir Shaivism.

Pt. Krishna Joo believes that spiritual bliss is realizable through the exercise of Yogic discipline. He is conscious of the fact that concentration can be achieved through Yogic discipline. He seeks divine grace for the purification of his mind and soul through Yoga. He prays for Lord Shiva's grace in directing his sense perceptions of the eternal truth of Advaita Vedantic monism. The saint-poet narrates the story of creation. According to him, Lord Shiva, from whom' illusory cosmos has originated is the master of the cosmos.

Pt. Krishna Joo Razdan celebrates the union of Shiva and Shakti in his Achhe Posh Gav Lachhi Novuy Heth. Here Shiva is Chandrachud appearing in dark fortnight and Uma is Param Shakti; here Shiva is Lachhinov and Uma is Achhe Posh. With the union of Shiva and Shakti, spring stalks the earth afresh and the cosmos blossoms like a lotus. Razdan Sahib is convinced that spiritual progress is realizable only through regular Yogic exercises.

He was a great Sadhak. He ended his journey of life at his birth place in 1926 and took Mahasamadhi there.

Bhagwan Gopi Nath (1898-1968)

Bhagwan Gopinath was born in a Kashmiri pandit family of Bhans, in a locality called Bhan Mohalla, in the city of Srinagar in Kashmir. He was a mystic saint of 20th century Kashmir in India. He spent most of his time meditating at various shrines in Kashmir.

He practiced some form of tantric spiritual practices. It is said that he practiced some technique of meditation that would seemingly help him control elements (called tattvas) like fire and water out of the total 36 such elements enumerated in Kashmir Shaivism. He started the practice while keeping himself in a dark room for many years. He was found talking to and directing invisible people at times.

Various parts of his body like his shoulders and knees were seen shuddering at times.

His devotees have found it difficult to classify his spiritual journey into a particular school of Indian philosophical thought. Its widely believed that he must have followed the tenets of trika doctrine of Advaita (non-dual) Kashmir Shaivism (in which, the Goddess Bhairavi-Aghoreshwari is enthroned above God Bhairava and is the main ideal of worship with Jnana (knowledge), Iccha (will) and Kriya (action) having had a dominating influence on him.

Once, while explaining the inter-relation of various spiritual disciplines in realizing God, he said: " think of Brahman (God without a form) as a tree and if one sits on any one of its branches (various spiritual disciplines), the same goal will be reached in each case."

Self-realization comes when one bids farewell to ones ego. Lust is the biggest impediment in one's spiritual development. A seeker must surrender onto guru's feet with all his heart and soul. One should always contribute to charity to not let greed settle in. In culture

Swami Gobind Kaul

Swami Gobind Kaul was born at Vanpoh in District Anantnag, Jammu and Kashmir State, India. He had association with many saints, particularly Swami Krishanjoo Razdan (his maternal uncle. Gobind Kaul' as a devotee began his spiritual journey to the Divine and in course of time, through sustained devotion and Sadhana, attained Self-realization.

He praises Siva as the light of pure Consciousness whose grace the devotees seek in having a spiritual bath in the Mansarovar (the tranquil lake of the mind). Gobind invokes the skull bearer, to bum his very marrow as his oven of love is fully ablaze. To Him, stationed in the temple of his heart, he would offer the flowers of love in worship. He naturally regards love as the very fountain-head of spirituality, the very source and culmination of life.

Swami Lakshmanjoo (1907-1991)

In the 20th century, Swami Lakshmanjoo, himself a Kashmiri Brahmin, helped revive both the scholarly and yogic streams of Kashmir Shaivism. His contribution is enormous. Lakshmanjoo approached Shaivism via knowledge first, and then experience. He inspired a generation of scholars who made Kashmir Shaivism a legitimate field of inquiry within the academy. The first stream of modern Kashmir Shaivism was established by Swami Lakshmanjoo of Ishbur, Srinagar, Jammu and Kashmir. He built a reputation as a scholar and as a yogi. According to him, Kashmir Shaivism springs from the direct visionary experience of the sages. Swami Lakshman Joo says:

One should concentrate on the state when sleep has not yet come, but the external awareness has disappeared (between waking and sleep) – there the supreme Goddess reveals herself.

Swami Lakshman Joo says of *yoga nidra* or "lucid dreaming". "You do not go in the dreaming state. You never sleep. It is that point which gives you rest and relaxation and that relaxation of going to sleep is because of entering through that channel. You are not aware of your body. The body is not there. You do not see your body, you do not see dreams, but you are aware of your being. The body is not sleeping actually. Every other person will observe you are in Samadhi. You do not see your body. You are conscious of the self only. But this is the real rest."

Either sitting on a seat or lying on a bed one should meditate on the body as being support less. When the minds becomes empty and support less, within a moment one is liberated from mental dispositions (the way that someone normally thinks and behaves).

Swami Lakshman Joo comments: "Imagine, you have thrown away the body as if it is nothing. There is no support for this body. Then, when thoughtlessness arises, the yogi enters in an instant in the thoughtless state of God consciousness."

Muktananda Parmahamsa (1908-1982)

The second stream of modern Kashmir Shaivism was inspired by Swami Muktananda Parmahamsa, who toured the world teaching the principles of Shaivism. His approach focused heavily on Sadhana and spiritual experience. Muktanandas Shaivism began with experience and then found understanding in the Shaivite scriptures. Muktananda had a significant impact among thousands of spiritual seekers. He transmitted the experience of Shaivism through the spiritual awakening of shaktipat. He spread Shaivite learning to many people. The goal of Kashmir Shaivism is to become divine.

Muktananda emphasized the importance of a self-realized guru who can awaken and guide the kundalini energy of a seeker.

Swami Shankarananda (1942)

Swami Shankarananda (born 1942) is an American-born guru. He is in the lineage of Bhagavan Nityananda of Ganeshpuri. The gurus of this lineage are noted for their reputation to be able to awaken the kundalini energy of seekers by means of shaktipat. Swami Shankarananda is an author and authority on the philosophy and practice of Kashmir Shaivism. He emphasizes spiritual practice (Sadhana), especially meditation, mantra and self-inquiry. He is a prominent spiritual teacher in Australia, where he founded the Shiva Ashram, a residential spiritual school where about 40 seekers live and members of the wider public visit for programs, and courses.

According to Swami Shankarananda, Consciousness is everything. Consciousness is the most intimate experience of life, the essence of life itself. Among the many spiritual traditions born and developed in India, one ancient philosophy-Kashmir Shaivism-has explored it completely. Until now, Kashmir Shaivism was a mysterious field. It was accessible only to a few scholars and other specialists. Here, for the first time, Swami Shankarananda, a Self-realized spiritual master, presented the wisdom of this powerful tradition of Kashmir Shaivism in a form that delighted and inspired all spiritual seekers of modern times. He explored the teachings in rich detail. He made Kashmir Shaivism easy to understand. He clarified the ideas and meditative practices of many great beings through wisdom and personal experience.

Shankarananda says that within every person there is a great power and a great potential that can be awakened by means of the grace of the guru and through spiritual practice. He came into contact with Kashmir Shaivism through his teacher, Swami Muktananda.

Shankarananda has described Kashmir Shaivism as a "philosophy of Consciousness", while Advaita Vedanta, and advocates the primacy of consciousness as the ground of all being. In contrast to Advaita Vedanta, however, Kashmir Shaivism regards unique or phenomenal reality as an expression or manifestation of consciousness, rather than Maya or illusion. He applies the teachings of Kashmir Shaivism to daily life and the practitioner's own experience. He has succeeded in making Kashmir's Shaiva Yoga come alive.

He practices and teaches Sadhana which includes meditation, chanting, repetition of the lineage mantra (Om Namah Shivaya), service, satsang and Self-inquiry.

Kashmir Shaivism can be summed up in one sentence: 'Everything is Chiti, everything is Consciousness'. All questions appear in Consciousness and nowhere else!

Of Her own free will, Chiti unfolds the universe on Her own screen. Consciousness creates the universe of Her own free will. Consciousness is free and Shiva unfolds the universe within Himself.

The subjective side of supreme consciousness is usually referred to as Shiva, and objective side as Shakhti. In fact they are one.

Chiti is sometimes considered the Goddess and is sometimes referred to as neutral consciousness.

Shaivism encourages to more thoughtful form of godly experience to the individual experience and back. It says that if you want to understand God, then know yourself. If you want to understand yourself, then understand God. But always look to your own experience first.

Consciousness is unique because every molecule, and every atom – that is talked about is consciousness that way replicates the whole. It is a hologram of everything. 'As above, so below.' Shaivism says, 'As here, so elsewhere,' as elsewhere, so here'.

Everything is contained in the minutest part.

Cosmology According to Kashmir Shaivism

(Special Features)

Param Shiva

a) Supreme self of pure consciousness surveys itself.

b) It is transcendental and extra cosmic reality.

c) This pure SUN of consciousness called Param Shiva has non-relational and immediate awareness of I. 'I' and 'the other' aspects of consciousness are in indistinguishable unity.

Shiva

a) Shiva is the changeless principle of all changes.
b) By its shining everything else shines.
c) Inter-cosmic, Immanent Reality, supporting dynamic energy in the background.
d) Container of everything.

Shakti

a) The dynamic energy aspect of Shiva as his I-consciousness.

b) If Shiva is the container, what is contained therein is his Shakti.

c) The sovereign Power to create.

d) Absolute bliss is her essential nature.

Sadashiva

a) The Sadashiva has power of the will to create.

b) In its experience as 'I' am this. The 'other' side, i.e., the universe to be, is quite hazy.

Ishwara

a) The power of knowledge is prominent here as 'the other' side of 'this am I' consciousness is quite distinct.

Shuddhavidya

a) The power of assuming every form.

b) 'I' and the 'other' are quite distinct and prominent but 'this' is still felt as part of the self.

Maya

a) The principle of delimitation; contracting infinite into finite.

b) The make-believe power of Nature, excluding 'the other' side of experience from the 'I' side of universal experience.

c) Maya draws a veil over the self owing to which he forgets his self. The five products of Maya are (i) Kala (ii) Vidya (iii) Raga (iv) Kaal (v) Niyati.

Pursha and Prakriti

Shiva under the influence of Maya loses his universal nature, and becomes a limited individual soul. Subjective side of Shiva under the influence of Maya is Purusha and its objective side is Prakriti.

Kashmir Shaivism and Modern Science

The philosophy of Vedic religion [HIDUISM] that this universe is Maya is being criticized on this ground, that this world is real as it produces phenomenon. But Vedanta clearly states that this world is illusion [MAYA]. This Maya is neither real nor unreal. It is not real because it ceases to exist when BRAHMAN is realized. Maya is cause of Creation; BRAHMAN is the nominal cause for creation. It is also substantial cause and undifferentiated cause for creation. Veil caused by Maya is of two types: covering truth and projection [appearing to be true].

Creator is both intelligent and material cause of this Universe. He cannot be outside Universe, and then He will have to create outside Universe. He cannot be inside Universe as it will be limited by Creation, so He and Creation cannot be separated. If Creation is infinite, so must be Creator. Every action involves triad of Actor, Action and acting, each one limits the other. Vedanta says consciousness is BRAHMAN and not BRAHMAN is consciousness. That means consciousness is, therefore, both a necessary and sufficient qualification for BRAHMAN.

Objects in world are fundamentally made from electrons protons, neutrons, assembled in different ways. Essentially we come to a limiting case where observation of the fundamental material content depends on observer, a conscious entity. The implication is-------that investigation of fundamental blocks of Universe is futile unless one takes in to consideration the role of Consciousness. Is this world real or unreal------answer depends on from what point of reference the question is asked. From the point of view of carpet salesman, Carpet is real. But from point of view of Chemist, there no material called Carpet; even while he is paying high price for carpet that he is buying.

BRAHMAN is sentient and world is insentient [inert]. Brahman is Nirgun [Vaishnav's say has attributes]. So existence of world is due to Conscious entity as inert world cannot prove its existence. It is conscious entity which says world exists. This world is a lower level of reality. From

absolute point of view, there is only Brahman--------
Existence, Consciousness and limitless.

I am not located in space but space is located in me since I can exist without space, but space cannot exist without me ----Sri Krishna in Bhagwat Gita"

So in nutshell Vedanta says that Creator and Created are one and same.

Now let us examine this from scientific view.

Science confirms that reality we see is an illusion------Our 3D Universe is a hologram. It is brain which receives signals and organizes these into a hologram, which we project outside and call it a reality.

Matter does not exist, what exists is intelligence. There is no such thing as this and that electron. It exists only in relation to other. It has no locality. This world is a tiny tiny frequency range within an infinite energy range. At deeper level [subatomic level] everything dissolves and what remains is just relationship. It is an act of consciousness which creates building block of which Universe is made. Consciousness is programming language of this Universe.

From nothing----came Consciousness, Energy, Space, MIND, time and later Matter. All Matter is nothing but energy. Atom only appears in a particular place if you measure it [observe it].Atoms are spread all over place. Matter is nothing but energy which is in vibration.

There are parallel Universes. There could be a universe without intelligence. If computer speed in future is extremely fast, one could recreate ones past hologram, and then it might become difficult to know which is real and which is virtual.

Quantum mechanics showed that predictions of science are probabilistic. Physicists agree that we encounter a single definite reality but there is no consensus amongst them as to how this basic fact is compatible with the theory's mathematical expression. String theory means different Universes with different laws of physics.

Many people agree that it is in India where the science of sound has achieved its highest level of scientific verification. The Kashmir Shaivism tradition has investigated sound with scientific rigor parallel to that of modern physics. Elaborate texts have created a complex terminology to describe their experiences with sound[*1]. The conclusion is that the universe emanates from sound, especially from a specific subtle sound out of which all vibrations emerge. The tradition also states that matter proceeds from vibrations. It describes a kind of hierarchy of sound in which the subtle incorporates the dense. "Differing from other forms of hierarchies, (The Shaivism tradition) recognizes no separation among levels. The subtlest incorporates the densest. A human being without preparation is only aware of denser levels. In the same way that melody played in violin disappears if it occurs at the same time as the sound of a train, the awareness of subtlest sound, the subtlest vibration, gets lost within the distracted consciousness of an unprepared mind [*2]"

The two most important discoveries that Kashmir Shaivism has revealed can be summarized in two points:

Sound (as vibration) is the essence of universe.

To comprehend sound is a path to self-realization and liberation[*3].

The premise of Kashmir Shaivism that vibration is the essence of the universe, and the Sufi premise that sound is the ground of being from which all form manifests itself have both been already confirmed by modern science.

The work of Swiss natural scientist, artist, and physician Hans Jenny (1904-1972) has contributed significantly to an understanding of how sound manifests form. His work, known as cymatics, studies wave from phenomena, or how vibrations in the broadest sense generate and influence patterns, shapes, and organic processes.

The premise of Kashmir Shaivism, that to comprehend sound is the path to self- realization.

Modern research has shown interest in the science of studying consciousness. With a better understanding of neurological functioning, ground work for new approach to understanding spiritual experiences is possible. Have we finally the point where we can reintegrate spirituality and science?

Consciousness has long been considered a missing link that might help us understanding many phenomena that still seem fragmented or not integrated. Consciousness can provide the link that unites fragments into a holographic vision of the world, demonstrating once and for all consciousness is a holographic reality of our brain.

In the Tibetan tradition, just as in the Sufi, exercises in the overtones are considered to be most spiritual manifestation of sound. Tibetan tantric chants, for example, use extremely frequency sounds and, most unusual, produce more than one tone simultaneously with the voice. Each chanter produces a chord that contains the second and third harmonics (up to the 10th harmonics) above the fundamental. These sounds enhance the immune system by producing chemical and electrical transformations in the body say the knowledgeable Buddhists.

Close analysis of both Vedanta and scientific thoughts shows tremendous similarities. Great Einstein said long back----"-Religion without science is blind, Science without religion is lame."

To summarize, Shaivism and modern science have a lot of commonalities:--

Shaivism

1. Consciousness (Shiva) is both intelligent and material cause of this Universe.

2. This Universe is superimposition on consciousness (Shiva). It involutes and evolves.

3. Time and space are in consciousness.

4. There are multiple Universes (14).

5. Matter is both manifestation and manifest.

6. Space /time travel possible with Sadhana.

7. Time travels with different speeds to different observers.

Science

1. Singularity (Primal matter) is cause of this Universe

2. Singularity (primal matter) is expanding and cooling expansion will be followed by dissolution.

3. Time and Space are in Singularity and not vice-versa.

4. Multiple Universes++.

5. There is Matter, Anti matter, Dark matter.

6. Space/time travel possible in far distant future.

7. Time speed variable in different Galaxies.

Science which started with a belief that everything we believe should be scientifically verifiable finds itself on threshold of uncertainty. Quantum physics dealing at subatomic levels, acknowledges its various surmises are probabilistic. It also acknowledges that matter has no locality, what really exists is intelligence. It is this intelligence which is called Consciousness (SHIVA) by Shaivites. One can find more and more similarities in science and Shaivism if we burrow deeper in these two philosophies. It is quite obvious that science probes outer space to know the Truth and religions have been probing inner space (SELF) to know the Truth.

Just as science cannot explain where from its Singularity came, in same way religions cannot say where from God (SHIVA) came.

Abrahamic Religions, Vedanta and Kashmir Shaivism

What is Vedanta?

Vedanta is derived from two words, *Veda* knowledge and *anta* end. Vedanta means culmination (peak, height, zenith, conclusion) of knowledge. It is the ancient Indian philosophy which answers the fundamental questions of life. Founded on no individual, it is a system of knowledge discovered by pre-eminent seekers of Truth. The knowledge promotes material and spiritual wellbeing. It introduces the higher values of service to provide peace and prosperity to the community. Above all, its philosophy leads one to the ultimate goal of Self - Realization. Vedanta is one of the six orthodox schools of Hindu philosophy. Vedanta literally means "end of the Vedas", reflecting ideas that emerged from the theories and philosophies contained in the Upanishads.

Hinduism is a Dharmic religion, while Judaism, Christianity, and Islam are sometimes called Abrahamic religions because they all accept the tradition of a god, Yahweh, that revealed himself to the prophet Abraham.

Abraham is traditionally considered to be the first Jew and to have made a promise with God. Because Judaism, Christianity, and Islam all recognize Abraham as their first prophet, they are also called the Abrahamic religions.

All Abrahamic religions claim to be monotheistic, worshiping an exclusive God, although one known by different names.

Abrahamic religions are religions that believe in Abraham being a prophet of God. They believe that there is only one God, and that He is supreme. Humans are separate from God and are inherently sinful. They must atone for their sins by following the path set out for them in their holy scriptures. In fact, another key characteristic of Christianity and Islam is that they both have just one set of official scriptures. For Christianity, it is the Bible and for Islam it is the Quran. Christianity and Islam are based on a philosophy of salvation, and they both are exclusivist religions. The philosophy of salvation here means that the religion centers around saving one's soul from going to Hell through worship of God. They are exclusivist because they claim that you MUST convert to their religion to attain Heaven, or else you will be eternally punished. Hinduism is very different in almost every aspect. Hinduism, along with Buddhism, Jainism, and Sikhism, is a Dharmic religion. In Hinduism, humans are one with God, not inherently sinful. God encompasses everything, opposed to the Abrahamic religions' strong boundaries on holy and unholy. Hinduism states that humans are reincarnated many times, the same soul inside many bodies.

The most prolific Hindu scriptures are the Vedas and the Bhagwat Gita. The Vedas contain detailed information for Vedic religion and rituals, while the Gita provides a commentary on Dharma, the concept of duty, and how to live life.

Christianity and Islam have the concept of one life – you have one life to attain salvation before God. This stands in stark contrast to Hinduism's reincarnation philosophy. Hinduism also has a multitude of deities, while Abrahamic religions have only one. There are countless Hindu scriptures, each with a unique take on Hinduism. That is why Hinduism is split into many different forms, such as Vaishnavism and Shaivism. Shaivism itself has a multitude of different branches as well, with Kashmir Shaivism being one of them.

Though there is evidence of existence of Advaita tradition prior to Shankaracharya, but the credit of authoritative explanation and popularization of Advaita goes to Adi Shankaracharya. Advaita is a sub-school of Vedanta.

An unplanned reader may not be able to make out the differences in the philosophy of Kashmir Shaivism and Vedanta. However, careful analysis and reading will disclose the commonalties and the differences.

A) Common Concepts

The common concepts of Vedanta and Kashmir Shaivism may be summarized as follows:

- Consciousness (Chit)
- Both recognize consciousness as Supreme Reality. Vedanta calls it Parmatma whereas Shaivites call it Parmshiva.
- Cyclic nature of eternity
- Both believe in the cyclic nature of eternity that consists of vast phases of creation, preservation, and their dissolution.
- Bound Soul
- Both accept the belief that life and death are but two phases of a single cycle to which soul is bound.
- Moksha
- Both accept that knowledge is the path of freedom and yoga as the method of attaining liberation.
- Dharma

Both accept dharma as the moral law of universe that accounts for these eternal cycles of nature as well as the destiny of human soul in its evolution.

B) Some of the points of disagreement are:

1. Advaita Vedanta explains the problem of remarkable existence on the basis of two things. The first is known as Brahman (pure consciousness) and the second Avidya (inexplicable ignorance).

Kashmir Shaivism does not agree with the concept of Avidya to explain the remarkable existence. Abhinavgupta in his treatise on Kashmir Shaivism, disproves this concept.

2. Vedanta states that phenomenal universe we live in is not real. It only appears as an existent reality. It is other than what it seems e.g. like a rope mistaken for a snake. It is like a dream or a mirage – Vivarta. Brahman exists but appears falsely as God, finite soul (Purusha) and insentient (lifeless) matter (prakriti).

Abinavgupta contradicts these assumptions by stating "how can it be unreal when it is manifested. An object that appears clearly and creates the whole universe must be something real and substantial and should be described as such".

3. The one creative force out of which everything emerges is known as Ultimate Reality. According to Vedanta,

Brahman (chit) is the Ultimate Reality, while Kashmir Shaivism calls this Ultimate Reality as Parmshiva. Brahman is believed to have no activity (kriya.) It is the knowledge (prakash or jnana). As per Kashmir Shaivism, Parmshiva is knowledge (prakash/jnana) plus activity (kriya or vimarsha). Vedanta consider activity (kriya) residing only in the empirical subject (Jiva) and not in Brahman. Shivites on the other hand think that Vedanta takes kriya in a very narrow sense whereas it should be taken in a wider sense.

They argue that even knowledge (jnana) is an activity (kriya) of the Divine, without activity chit or the Divine Being would be inert and incapable of bringing about anything, least of all the whole cosmos. Parmshiva is svatantra (has free will) and therefore is a Karta (doer). Knowledge (jnana) is not a passive state of consciousness but an activity of consciousness, though an effortless one.

4. Manifestation of cosmos as per Kashmir Shaivism is called "Descent" – which means descent of cosmic self (Parmshiva) to a limited self (Jiva). Vedanta explains this process of manifestation through 25 elements. Kashmir Shaivism explains the cosmic evolution through 36 elements (tattvas) which include 23 elements of Vedanta without modification, 2 with modification, and prescribes 11 more elements (tattvas).

Parmshiva of Kashmir Shaivism is not the same Shiva of Vedanta who is meditating at Mount Kailash with Parvati by His side. Parmshiva is a Being, not necessarily in physical sense, who is Absolute, pure, eternal, infinite, and totally free I-consciousness whose essential nature is vibrant creative energy which Kashmir Shaivism describes as wonderful spiritual stir of blissfulness known as spanda. This spanda causes Absolute Reality to be continuously inclined towards the outward and joyful manifestation of its creative energy – Shakti. This manifestation is brought about by the freewill play (leela) of Parmshiva Himself like a childs' play that is without motivation. The outward divine manifestation of this creative energy appears in five activities:

1. The activity of creation.

2. The activity of preservation.

3. The activity of dissolution of all the elements including the beings living in them.

4. The activity of self-oblivion.

5. The activity of self-recognition of these created beings.

Stages 1,2,3 are common to both Kashmir Shaivism as well as Vedanta. However, Stages 4 and 5 listed above are present in Kashmir Shaivism only.

Three important observations to highlight the differences in the manifestation philosophies of Vedanta and Kashmir Shaivism are:

a) Purusha

While the Purusha of Vedanta is a Universal soul (God-like), He is atmen (pure spirit). In contrast, in Kashmir Shaivism it is bound soul – a jiva, nara, pashu or anu – a limited soul.

b) Prakriti

Prakriti in Vedanta is involved in manifestation as an independent element. It is a cosmic substance that is termed as perennial impulse in nature (like Shakti tattva). But the Prakriti of the Kashmir Shaivism deals with limited jiva only.

c) Maya

Maya in the Vedanta is the means of operation. It is not an element. It is force that creates the illusion of non-perception in nature. It has no reality. It is only the appearance of fleeting forms which are all unreal and like mirage vanishes when the knowledge of reality draws. In contrast, in Kashmir Shaivism maya is a tattva. It is real. It is the power of contraction or limiting the nature of five universal modes of consciousness. It cannot be separated from Absolute Reality – Parmshiva.

The defining characteristic of Kashmir Shaivism is its rich history. In ancient times, Kashmir was a center of learning. Kashmir Shaivism itself began around 1500 years ago: much after the original beginning of Shaivism. Religious ideas from around India swirled in the cultural melting pot.

People came to Kashmir seeking knowledge and truth, and for some of them, they found it in Kashmir Shaivism. Sometime in the 9th century, there lived a sage called Vasugupta. He lived on Mount Mahadev near Srinagar. One night, Shiva came to him in a dream, revealing the hiding place of the ancient philosophies. Vasugupta went to the place described and found many scriptures engraved on rocks. He named them "Shiva Sutras" and revealed them to his disciples. Thus, Kashmir Shaivism began to spread once more when Vasugupta taught his disciples two things which make up the core of Kashmir Shaivism philosophy: how to become fully divine and how to become fully human. He declared that Man's consciousness is Atman – his soul – and his soul *is* Shiva. In his writings, Vasugupta described the limitless power of awareness.

Kashmir Shaivism - a blend of two separate philosophies

Kaula and *Trika.*

1. *Kaula* is a Sanskrit word meaning community, family, and totality. Kaula philosophy inspires a family-based way of life, emphasizing the importance of community. Kashmir Shaivism recommended a *'secret'* performance of

Kaula practices in keeping with its heritage. This was to be done in seclusion from public eyes, therefore, allowing one to maintain the appearance of a typical householder. Since Kashmir Shaivism has the concepts of Kaula at its core, a sense of community is fostered, and no renunciation is necessary. In fact, Kashmir Shaivites are encouraged to lead a healthy householder's life. Nonviolence is also an important part of Kashmir Shaivism. Other branches of Shaivism lead their followers to commit atrocities in the name of Shiva, but Kashmir Shaivism never encouraged that – which ties in to the Kaula aspects of Kashmir Shaivism.

2. *Trika* is a Sanskrit word meaning three, or trinity. Trika says that everything in the Universe is in three forms, like Shiva's trident, the three forms being Shiva as God, Shakti as the Creative Energy, and Anu as the individual. Abhinavgupta, a 10th century sage, gave Kashmir Shaivism its modern shape by combining the teachings of Kaula and Trika. Abhinavgubta's teachings say that Shiva *is* the universe and that Shiva is consciousness, also known as Chit. The universe is made from Shiva's awareness, and we

are here due to Shiva's will. The universe is created by Shiva extending his will and restored to tranquility by withdrawing it. One of Kashmir Shaivism's key characteristics is that there is no concept of enlightenment through renunciation, unlike many Dharmic religions.

The *Trika* system of Kashmir Shaivism explains the nature and cause of bondage and means to liberation. Trika is a Sanskrit word meaning three, or trinity. Therefore, the three main divisions of Kashmir Shaivism are:

i) **The Agama Shastra** – (Sadhna Shastra) It mainly deals with ritualistic and mystic practices.

ii) **The Spanda Shastra** –(Energy) ; [The vibrations.]- Spanda describes the power of consciousness which infuses and permeates life into physical senses. The basic idea is that Shiva's Spanda (energy) out of its own self. According to this doctrine world is a play of energy force or vibration.

iii) **The Pratyabhijna Shastra** - (Recognition). This school of Kashmir Shaivism existed before the time of Asoka (273-232 B.C.). 'Pratyabhijna' is recognition. It knows the sense of awareness, consciousness, realization, 'knowledge in practice' and practical use of knowledge.

Pratyabhijna school thinks that man is ignorant and unaware of the very nature of one's own Self (Shiva-Atman), viz. his inner being. The man is ignorant about great sense within him, and its power of *Will, knowledge, Thought* and *Action*, viz., man's abilities with which he is gifted by fate. The school believes that the abilities, with which man is born in this world, comprise his supreme (divine) inheritance.

Pratyabhijna is, in its essence, a deep and systematic study of man as small, and the world he lives in as big. The Pratyabhijna is directed to removing the veil of ignorance from us and turning our attention towards the deeper faculties within us. Pratyabhijna lays emphasis on human values and basic virtues. According to Pratyabhijna, human beings are by nature divine. They are the sparks of the divine, children of God. The whole mankind forms one family. It is by self-discipline (culture) and clean moral life that man can unveil the divine qualities in his personality. Love of God in this school means love of human beings. He, who loves God, loves everybody and looks on all men as equals. Love of God is to be translated into service of one's fellow – men.

Gentleness, morality, sympathy, openness and honest dealings with one another are qualities or virtues necessary for good life. Pratyabhijna promotes the values of peace and freedom and human dignity beneficial to the common man.

These values are stated in precious terms like :

a) **Sarva-shivata** - which signifies that the personality of every human individual is divine or sacred.

b) **Sarva-samata**- meaning that all men are born equal, and

c) **Sarva - svatantrya** - i.e. all men are born free. And above all,

d) **Vishva-Shanti**.- Pratyabhijna directs man to work for peace and tranquility of the world - Following the truth is conducive to the good and benefit of the whole humanity, and so on. Thus the doctrine lays emphasis on 'liberty, equality and fraternity' which is the famous motto of 'the civilized world today.

Kashmir was the cradle of Shaivism. The Prakriti (nature) provided the symbolic representation of Lord Shiva in the higher reaches of the valley on the mountains like Harmukh and Mahadev.

Shiva under the influence of Maya (The make-believe power of Nature) loses his universal nature, and becomes a limited individual soul. Subjective (Individual) side of Shiva under the influence of Maya is *Purusha* and its objective side is *Prakriti*. Shiva maintains himself as universe through his cosmic energy Shakti, who is inseparable from him. At the temporal level, these two cosmic principle, one mystical and the other inherent, are represented by male and female principal. Shivas consider all females as manifestation of Shakthi, they regard woman as equal to man so far as her social position is concerned. Even today in a Kashmiri Pandit marriage the bridegroom and the bride are worshipped as Shiva and Shakhti.

The bhakta's attitude is that God is great and he is small. (bhakta is a Sanskrit word which means a religious devotee or a believer). But Shaivism's stance is much bolder. It says that you are not the little bhakta who says, 'God is great, I am small' You are Shiva Himself. Shaivism invites you to contemplate 'I am Shiva, here and now.'

This room I am in exists for me because I am here. When I go to sleep at night my outer world ceases to exist. When I open my eyes the world exists again for me. When Shiva opens His eyes, the universe is created. When He closes His eyes it disappears. You will never have a universe beyond your own awareness. Thus, you are the aware subject of the universe you experience. You are Shiva.

Finally, I salute that Shiva that lives in every one of you, my readers, as your own awareness. Remember, Shiva lives in every thought and feeling, in every breath, in every object, and in every person. The highest, most truly worthy expression of our common humanity is the search for the self within.

Kashmir Shaivism is the study of consciousness. Since consciousness is infinite, so our study is without limits. Consciousness is one no matter where we find it, though its personalities are many. Kashmir Shaivism says that if we could pare away that superficial layer and know ourselves as we truly are, we would discover ourselves as divine beings, Shiva Himself.

In nut shell it may be said that Vedanta says only consciousness is real; and the world is unreal! Swami Shankaracharya of South says only self is real, and the whole world is unreal! Whereas the shrewd, smart and perceptive Yogis of Kashmir say that the world is real, but it is made up of consciousness. This was a breakthrough in Kashmir Shaivism. According to Kashmir Shaivism this world is real, but it is a play and expression of consciousness. Your dream is an expression of your consciousness. The Trika philosophy of Kashmir Shaivism provided relationship between God, nature, and man. It also provided the philosophy of Shiv-Shakti and Nara (man), which forms the main philosophy of all Shaivic philosophies. Kashmir Shaivism is both a philosophy and yoga. It is a philosophy of salvation. It discusses Sadhana, meditation techniques and understandings that are useful today. Kashmir Shaivism can be summed up in one sentence: 'Everything is Consciousness (Chit),'. All questions appear in Consciousness and nowhere else!

Consciousness is embarrassment to western science and philosophy. Darwinism, too, is weak when it comes to consciousness. How did this miracle we know as our own awareness suddenly spring into being from amino acids via natural selection? Darwinians don't want to look too deeply at this question. Science does not actually address the issue of consciousness. Science acknowledges consciousness, but avoids the question of what it is and where it came from.

When Kashmir Shaivism is studied it becomes a set of principles and concepts. The rich concepts are not only food for the intellect, but also implies direct nurturance of soul, the direct experience of consciousness itself.

In Shaiva-Yoga the guidance of a sat-guru, a perfect soul, is a must. The Shaiva-texts describe a sat-guru as one who initiates, teaches and showers grace (Shaktipat). For the disciple a sat-guru is Shiva Himself. Guru, to Khemraj, is the means to realisation (Shiva-Sutra). A disciple has to be insightful and receptive to what sat-guru teaches him. Sat-guru and disciple are in a relation of identity.

Reason in Shaiva-Yoga is not at all considered as extraneous. Right reason is a real aid in learning and grasping the subtleties of Shaiva-thought. It plays a positive role in cleansing the head and heart of a seeker. Sharp intellect tempers an aspirant for the quest. The world-view that Kashmir Shaivism projects as its essence needs a reason-based comprehension and appreciation. Hence, reason, to Kashmir Shaivism, is a valued asset for a seeker undertaking a spiritual journey.

Scriptures pertaining to the domain of Shaivism and other forms of thought-structures are receptacle of all the distilled knowledge that has come right from Shiva Himself; God reveals Himself through them (scriptures). They are one of the forms in which He, (Shiva) is directly apparent in this world'. The scriptures teach, reveal, define and describe what is worth to be sought after. The scriptural knowledge as wisdom has to be translated into experiential knowledge through the Shaiva customs and established practices. What is highly significant about Kashmir Shaivism is that it is so inclusive that it does not reject any method and form of spiritual discipline of indigenous origins that helps in the expansion of consciousness (unmesh) of a seeker. Any method that suits the abilities and psychic-frame of a seeker can be practised to cognise his original status of Shiva. Methods or means are many in number. Their worthiness and usefulness as a tool are determined by the spiritual goals that a seeker pursues.

In Kashmir Shaivism one finds a special Shakti, or powerful spiritual energy, unique to Kashmir Shaivism. Shakti loves Shaivism and she never fails to show up.

In one of her vakhs, Lal Ded says -I freed myself of all the emotional outbursts; I killed my desires; then, I achieved all my purpose and came to be known Lalla; and- I achieved all my purpose only when I devoted myself wholly to my Lord Shiva.

Mal vonda zolum,

Jigar (kam) morum

Teli lalla nav draam

Yeli dali travimas tattie

Lal Ded says that she surrendered herself entirety to His grace. Shiva's unlimited powers of thought and action obscures the connection between universal consciousness and individual consciousness. Human ignorance results from three particular limitations of consciousness. Shiva's power of intentionality condenses into the individual (anava) will, his omniscience becomes subject to illusion (maya), and his universal action becomes bound to the limited action of individual selves (karma).

The *three* impurities are known as *'maya', ' karma' and 'anava'*. Maya and karma need to be consumed and removed in the glowing fire of yoga. Anava mal as such cannot be removed through any form of Yoga. It needs Shiva's grace.

The *anavamala, is the projection of consciousness from its universal source onto an individual (anava) center of consciousness. It gives beings with differential insights and understandings so that they experience themselves as separate individuals.*

These three limitations are also known as the 'malas' or "impurities," which obscure consciousness and prevent a person from realizing one's true nature. When alive, the powers of the human being become restricted within the individual mental processes, senses and actions, all of which reinforce a sense of separateness between self and others and between self and the true self, Shiva.

Lal Ded reflects upon the power of each of the three 'malas' to block spiritual realization. The 'malas' are spots or smudges on the mirror of identity; they prevent the self from seeing the self within. She says: When my mind like dust from a mirror got removed from all impurities; the knowledge came to me that He was everything and I nothing.

Identification with the embodied personality is "nothing" compared to the all - encompassing "everything" of the universal subject. Liberation comes when we cease to identify ourselves in a limited manner.

Kashmir Shaivism vigorously affirms the reality of creation. Maya is not illusion; the world really exists. Maya does, however, impede the human mind from seeing beyond worldly diversity to its source.

Gently and gently shall I weep for you, O Mind

You have been caught under the spell of delusion

Even shadow of the worldly possession will not stand by you

Alas, You have lost your own identity!

Sahaj resides at the very core of the great saint and poetess Lal Ded of Kashmir.

Shiv is Sakala -With form, such as Maheshwara

Shiv is Nishkala – Without form such as Brahman

Shiv is Asciatic- A hermit

Shiv is Erotic- pleasure, desire

Shiv is Purusha - Human being

Shiv is Prakriti- nature

Shiv is Aughardani- hermit by itself but bountiful for others.

Conclusion

Kashmiri Shaivism does not advocate a life of renunciation or profession of monks. It recommends an active householder's life with daily practice of worship, yoga and meditation. All other deities (gods and goddesses) of the traditional Hindu pantheon are worshipped as various manifestations of Shiva and Shakhti. Shaivism is a philosophy that recognizes and explains the universe as a manifestation of one divine, conscious energy. The Trika system of Kashmir Shaivism, explains the nature and cause of bondage and the means to liberation. It describes how the yogi who remains alert can perceive the divine vibration, or spanda, in all moments of daily life, thus regaining the vision of unity-consciousness.

Kashmir Shaivism holds that it is by the grace of God (Saktipata)--in the form of the grace of the master--that Lord Shiva is revealed. The goal of Kashmir Shaivism is to merge in Shiva or Universal Consciousness, or realize one's already existing identity with Shiva, by means of wisdom, yoga and grace. "Kashmir Shaivism has penetrated to that depth of living thought where diverse currents of human wisdom unite in a luminous synthesis.

The life in the Kashmir valley taught the philosophers a simple, yet detailed path to reach the ultimate purpose of life. Kashmir Saivism is intensely monistic. It does not deny the existence of a personal God or of the Gods. But much more emphasis is put upon the personal meditation and reflection of the devotee and his guidance by a guru.

Kashmir Saivism embraces both knowledge and devotion. Sadhana leads to the assimilation of the object (world) in the subject (I) until the Self (Siva) stands revealed as one with the universe. The goal-liberation-is sustained recognition (Pratyabhijna) of one's true Self as nothing but Siva. There is no merger of soul in God, as they are eternally no different.

Kashmir Shaivism is a universal system, pure, real, and substantial in every respect, which can be practiced by everyone. A Shiva follower wakes up early and takes a bath. He applies ash on the forehead and lights a lamp before the Shiva idol. Then he offers some flowers or Bel leaves which Shiva loves. Then a Shivalinga is given a bathe it with water, and Bhasma or Ash is applied by Shiva devotees as the tilak.

In the 20th century, Swami Lakshmanjoo, a Kashmiri Brahmin, helped revive both the scholarly and yogic streams of Kashmir Shaivism.

In nut shell, Kashmir Shaivism is both a philosophy and yoga. It is a philosophy of salvation. It discusses Sadhana, meditation techniques and understandings that are useful today.

Kashmir Shaivism can be summed up in one sentence: 'Everything is Chiti, Everything is Consciousness." 'The self is consciousness.' The nature of reality is consciousness,' or, everything is consciousness."

The Kashmir Shaivism also has important Tantric influences. Here, just as in Tantrism, we find the idea that all things are mysteriously and closely interconnected, as in a holographic model of the universe. Thus, the whole universe is envisaged as a gigantic net of virtual resonances that are established between each point (atom) of the universe and all the other points (atoms). Knowing in-depth one single aspect (atom) of the universe, we are then able to know the entire universe, because all is resonance. At this stage, resonance is a concept more and more debated, of a growing importance in our contemporary culture and science.

The name of Kashmir at once brings to the mind the vision of a beautiful valley nested deep in The Himalayas. Standing majestically in its mountain isolation, Kashmir has been crucible for refining human thought, be it Shaivism, Buddhism or Sufism.

"Kashmir Shaivism" is supreme. It was brought to the knowledge of the world outside of Kashmir by Georg Buhler in his report published in 1877. He was in Search of Sanskrit manuscripts in Kashmir, Rajputana and Central India then. In 1911 a Research Department was set up by the government of Pratap Singh Sahib Bahadur, Maharaja of Jammu and Kashmir with Mukund Ram Shastra as its head pandit. Under its auspices the Kashmir Series of Texts and Studies was published starting in 1911 and extending into the 1960's, but with the last volume related to Kashmir

Shaivism being published in 1947. Thus, the core texts of the non-dual Shaivism of Kashmir were published. Many books were published from manuscripts in the personal possession of the pandits of the Research Department.

The Kashmiri Pandits the main votaries of Shaivism have been the main targets of terrorism. They had to flee from their home and hearth. In other words Shaivism is now under siege. Today we think of Kashmir as a battlefield, but a thousand years ago it was a haven of religious tolerance where Kashmir Shaivism flourished in an atmosphere of respect.

Glossary

A creation myth (or cosmogonic myth) is a symbolic narrative of how the world began and how people first came to inhabit it. While in popular usage the term myth often refers to false or fanciful stories, members of cultures often ascribe varying degrees of truth to their creation myths. In the society in which it is told, a creation myth is usually regarded as conveying profound truths, metaphorically, symbolically and sometimes in a historical or literal sense. They are commonly, although not always, considered cosmological myths – that is, they describe the ordering of the cosmos from a state of chaos or amorphousness.

A deity - is a supernatural being considered divine or sacred. The Oxford Dictionary of English defines deity as "a god or goddess (in a polytheistic religion)", or anything revered as divine. C. Scott Littleton defines a deity as "a being with powers greater than those of ordinary humans, but who interacts with humans, positively or negatively, in ways that carry humans to new levels of consciousness, beyond the grounded preoccupations of ordinary life." A male deity is a god, while a female deity is a goddess.

A god is a male deity, in contrast with a goddess, a female deity. While the term "goddess" specifically refers to a female deity, the plural "gods" can be applied to deities collectively, regardless of gender.

A goddess is a female deity. Goddesses have been linked with virtues such as beauty, love, motherhood and fertility (Mother-goddess cult in prehistoric times). They have also been associated with ideas such as war, creation, and death. In some faiths, a sacred female figure holds a central place in religious prayer and worship. For example, Shaktism, the worship of the female force that animates the world, is one of the three major sects of Hinduism.

A pantheon - (from Greek, pantheon, literally "(a temple) of all gods", "of or common to all gods" . It is the particular set of all gods of any polytheistic religion, mythology, or tradition.

Abheda -non-dualism

Agama Shastra – (Sadhna Shastra) It mainly deals with ritualistic and mystic practices.

agamas- sacred writings

ananda -self-knowledge, it is the source of infinite delight

Asciatic- A hermit

Aughardani- Shiva is aughardani, i.e. hermit by itself but bountiful for others.

Bhakta - a believer, devotee, an admirer; bhakta is a Sanskrit word which means a religious devotee or a believer; bhaktas always desire love of God and they dedicate their actions to God. The glory of bhaktas is known only to themselves.

Bheda - dualism

Bheda- bheda -dualism-cum-non-dualism

Brahman (s) – From the Sanskrit brahmana, one of four major caste groups (varana) or social classes. Brahmans are the highest caste group, traditionally made up of priests, philosophers, scholars and religious leaders. Not to be confused with brahman (the Absolute Reality).

brahman – The Absolute Reality, the eternal, supreme, or ultimate principle. A state of pure transcendence. In some Vedantic schools of Hindu thought, a Supreme Being who is the cause of the universe, with theistic attributes. Not to be confused with Brahmin (the priestly class group). brahman is Nirgun [Vaishnav's say has attributes.

Brahman, in the Upanishads (Indian sacred writings), the supreme existence or absolute reality. The etymology of the word, which is derived from Sanskrit, is uncertain. Though a variety of views are expressed in the Upanishads, they concur in the definition of brahman as eternal, conscious, irreducible, infinite, omnipresent, and the spiritual core of the universe of finiteness and change. Marked differences in interpretation of brahman characterize the various schools of Vedanta, the system of Hindu philosophy based on the writings of the Upanishads.

According to the Advaita (Nondualist) school of Vedanta, brahman is categorically different from anything phenomenal, and human perceptions of differentiation are illusively projected on this reality. The Bhedabheda (Dualist-Nondualist) school maintains that brahman is nondifferent from the world, which is its product, but different in that phenomenality imposes certain adventitious conditions (upadhis) on brahman. The Vishishtadvaita (Qualified Nondualist) school maintains that a relation exists between brahman and the world of soul and matter that is comparable to the relation between soul and body; the school identifies brahman with a personal god, Brahma, who is both transcendent and immanent. The Dvaita (Dualist) school refuses to accept the identity of brahman and world, maintaining the ontological separateness of the supreme, which it also identifies with a personal god.

Chit - Shiva is the universe and that Shiva is consciousness, also known as Chit. According to Vedanta, Brahman (chit) is the Ultimate Reality, while Kashmir Shaivism calls this Ultimate Reality as Parmshiva.

Dualism is the belief proposed by Rene Descartes that the human mind and body are two distinct entities that interact with each other to make a person. Descartes reasoned that the mind and the body communicate with each other through a small structure at the base of the brain called the pineal gland. Dualism in Metaphysics is the belief that there are two kinds of reality: material (physical) and immaterial (spiritual). In Philosophy of Mind, Dualism is the position that mind and body are in some categorical way separate from each other, and that mental phenomena are, in some respects, non-physical in nature.

Erotic- pleasure

Guru – In Hinduism, a religious teacher or guide.

Iccha - Will

Invocation "to call on, invoke, to give" is a form of prayer, wherein one party humbly or earnestly asks another party to provide something, either for the party who is doing the supplicating (e.g., "Please spare my life.") or on behalf of someone else.

jati- Literally, birth group. Basic endogamous unit of caste system. There are nearly 3,000 'jatis' in contemporary society. The word jati is also sometimes used for ethnic, religious, or linguistic groups.

Jnana – knowledge

Jnana - knowledge, Thought

Kandas- sections

karma -Literally, action. Spiritual merit or demerit that a being acquired in a previous incarnation and is acquiring in present existence.

Kaula - Kaula is a Sanskrit word meaning community, family, and totality. Kaula philosophy inspires a family-based way of life, emphasizing the importance of community. Kashmir Shaivism recommended a 'secret' performance of Kaula practices in keeping with its heritage. This was to be done in seclusion from public eyes, therefore, allowing one to maintain the appearance of a typical householder.

Krama - In Sanskrit "process", "order", "controlled succession".

Kriya - Action, viz., man's abilities with which he is gifted by fate.

kriya- activity

Maya - The make-believe power of Nature, loses his universal nature, and becomes a limited individual soul. Subjective (Individual) side of Shiva under the influence of Maya is Purusha and its objective side is Prakriti. Shiva maintains himself as universe through his cosmic energy Shakhti, who is inseparable from him.

Moksha - salvation or liberation

Monism deals with oneness whereas dualism the concept of 'two'. ...Monism is the assumption that both mind and body are parts of one

Monotheism: It has been defined as the belief in the existence of only one god that created the world, is all-powerful and intervenes in the world. A broader definition of monotheism is the belief in one god. A distinction may be made between exclusive monotheism, and both inclusive monotheism and pluriform monotheism which, while recognizing various distinct gods, postulate some underlying unity.

mrityu -Death: The Sanskrit word for death is mrityu), which is often personified in Dharmic religions.

In Hindu scriptures, the lord of death is called King Yama, Yama Rājā). He is also known as the King of Karmic Justice (Dharmaraja) as one's karma at death was considered to lead to a just rebirth. (Yudhishthira, eldest of the pandavas and a personification of justice, was born through Kunti's prayers to Yama.) Yama rides a black buffalo and carries a rope lasso to carry the soul back to his home, called Naraka, pathalloka, or Yamaloka. There are many forms of reapers, although some say there is only one who disguises himself as a small child. His agents, the Yamadutas, carry souls back to Yamalok. There, all the accounts of a person's good and bad deeds are stored and maintained by Chitragupta. The balance of these deeds allows Yama to decide where the soul has to reside in its next life, following the theory of reincarnation. Yama is also mentioned in the Mahabharata as a great philosopher and devotee of the Supreme Brahman.

Nishkala – Without form such as Brahman

Objectivity is a philosophical concept, objective means being independent of the perceptions thus objectivity means the property of being independent from the perceptions, which has been variously defined by sources. Generally, objectivity means the state or quality of being true even outside a subject's individual biases, interpretations, feelings, and imaginings. A proposition is generally considered objectively true (to have objective truth) when its truth conditions are met without biases caused by feelings, ideas, opinions, etc., of a sentient subject. A second, broader meaning of the term refers to the ability in any context to judge fairly, without partiality or external influence. This second meaning of objectivity is sometimes used synonymously with neutrality.

Parmshiva - As per Kashmir Shaivism, Parmshiva is knowledge (prakash) plus activity (kriya).

Pleasure is a broad class of mental states that humans experience as positive, enjoyable, or worth seeking. It includes more specific mental states such as happiness, entertainment, enjoyment, ecstasy, and euphoria. The early psychological concept of pleasure, the pleasure principle, describes it as a positive feedback mechanism, motivating the organism to recreate in the future the situation which it has just found pleasurable and to avoid situations that have caused pain in the past.

The experience of pleasure is subjective and different individuals will experience different kinds and amounts of pleasure in the same situation. Many pleasurable experiences are associated with satisfying basic biological drives, such as eating, exercise, hygiene, and sex. The appreciation of cultural artifacts and activities such as art, music, dancing, and literature is often pleasurable.

Polytheism is the worship of or belief in multiple deities, which are usually assembled into a pantheon of gods and goddesses, along with their own religions and rituals. In most religions which accept polytheism, the different gods and goddesses are representations of forces of nature or ancestral principles, and can be viewed either as autonomous or as aspects or emanations of a creator deity or transcendental absolute principle (monistic theologies), which manifests immanently in nature (panentheistic and pantheistic theologies). Most of the polytheistic deities of ancient religions, with the notable exceptions of the Ancient Egyptian and Hindu deities, were conceived as having physical bodies.

Polytheism contrasts with monotheism, the belief in a singular God, in most cases superior. Polytheists do not always worship all the gods equally, but they can be specializing in the worship of one particular deity. Polytheism was the typical form of religion during the Bronze Age and Iron Age up to the Axial Age and the development of Abrahamic religions, the latter of which enforced strict Monotheism.

Prakash – knowledge

Prakriti- nature

Pratyabhijna - (Recognition). 'Pratyabhijna' is recognition. It knows the sense of awareness, consciousness, realization, 'knowledge in practice' and practical use of knowledge. **Pratyabhijna** school thinks that man is ignorant and unaware of the very nature of one's own Self (Shiva-Atman), viz. his inner being.

Prayer (from the Latin precari "to ask earnestly, beg, entreat") is an invocation or act that seeks to activate a rapport with an object of worship through deliberate communication.

Prayer can be a form of religious practice, may be either individual or communal and take place in public or in private. It may involve the use of words, song or complete silence. When language is used, prayer may take the form of a hymn, incantation, formal creedal statement, or a spontaneous utterance in the praying person. There are different forms of prayer such as petitionary prayer, prayers of supplication, thanksgiving, and praise. Prayer may be directed towards a deity, spirit, deceased person, or lofty idea, for the purpose of worshipping, requesting guidance, requesting assistance, confessing transgressions (sins) or to express one's thoughts and emotions. Thus, people pray for many reasons such as personal benefit or for the sake of others (called intercession).

Pursha - Human being

Sahaj- natural, It denotes both the nature of human being and the means for realizing it.

Sakala -With form, such as Maheshwara

sarva-samata - meaning that all men are born equal.

sarva-shivata - which signifies that the personality of every human individual is divine or sacred.

Sarva-svatantrya -(i.e. all men are born free.

Shuniya - *Shuniya or a zero point* is where the mind become still and you become the observer. Shuniya is a deep, meditative state of consciousness where the 'separate' self-identity softens into stillness. This state of being is so pure and clear that it is often referred to as a state of 'zero'. In Shuniya, the greater aspect of 'Self', or the 'higher self', is available and the experience of oneness is realized. The characteristics of Shuniya are inbuilt. The features of shuniya are graceful, soulful, neutral, sensual, accepting, and allowing. There is no judgment, expectation, opinion, pushing, or intellectualism. It is a pure form of love. In this state of consciousness, the Infinite is in charge and what happens is limitless.

Spanda Shastra – (Energy) ; [The vibrations.]-Spanda describes the power of consciousness which infuses and permeates life into physical senses. The basic idea is that Shiva's Spanda (energy) out of its own self. According to this doctrine world is a play of energy force or vibration.

Subjectivity is a philosophical concept, related to consciousness, agency, personhood, reality, and truth, which has been variously defined by sources. Three common definitions include that subjectivity is the quality or condition of: Something being a subject, narrowly meaning an individual who possesses conscious experiences, such as perspectives, feelings, beliefs, and desires. Something being a subject, broadly meaning an entity that has agency, meaning that it acts upon or wields power over some other entity (an object).

Supplication or prayer As a supplication or prayer it implies to call upon God, a god, goddess, or person, etc. When a person calls upon God, a god, or goddess to ask for something (protection, a favour, his/her spiritual presence in a ceremony, etc.) or simply for worship, this can be done in a pre-established form or with the invoker's own words or actions. All religions in general use invoking prayers, or hymns; for example the mantras in Hinduism and Buddhism.

Sutra - A sutra is a short aphoristic (saying) statement. Sutra (Sanskrit) comes from root word 'Siv', to sew, and is connected to English suture. So it is like a 'stich' or a 'thread' in the fabric of yogic knowledge. Sometimes poetic, sometimes enigmatic (mysterious) sentences – or fragments of sentence.

Tattvas - elements

Trika- Trika is a Sanskrit word meaning three, or trinity. Trika says that everything in the Universe is in three forms, like Shiva's trident, the three forms being Shiva as God, Shakti as the Creative Energy, and Anu as the individual. Trika philosophy of Kashmir Shaivism provided relationship between God, nature, and man. It also provided the philosophy of Shiv-Shakti and Nara (man), which forms the main philosophy of all Shaivic philosophies.

Tryambaks – They laid the foundations of the Kashmir Shaivism

Twice -born: Referring to jatis, claiming membership in one of the three upper varanas, that is, Brahman, Kshatriya, and Vaishya. Male members natural birth is followed by a spiritual rebirth in a rite involving investiture with a sacred thread.

Ultimate Reality - The one creative force out of which everything emerges is known as Ultimate Reality. According to Vedanta, Brahman (chit) is the Ultimate Reality – Brahman is believed to have no activity (kriya.) It is the knowledge (prakash or jnana). While Kashmir Shaivism calls this Ultimate Reality as Parmshiva.

Upayas-mystical practices (upayas) for achieving lower and higher Siddhi (supernatural powers) and the glories of life.

Varna- Literally, color. One of the four large caste groups (Brahman, Kshatriya, Vaisha, and Sudra) from which most jatis are believed to derive.

vimarsha- to know itself

vimarsha- to know itself

Vishva-Shanti - To work for peace and tranquility of the world.

About the Authors

Sham S. Misri

Born, brought up, educated, lived and married in Kashmir, one of the beautiful places in the world. In my mind this best place in the world is Mother Kashmir, which is what I call home. Everyone knows everyone because we have the same mother.

I did my Master's degree in Science from Kashmir University with high score. Initially worked in D.A.V. College, Jawahar Nagar, Srinagar, Jammu &Kashmir as a lecturer where I was familiar with the children and the staff. I later on switched over my job to Central services where I joined as a scientist, and retired from the same organization as Deputy Director, a senior level officer. Over the years of my active career there has been contributed to the cause of Education and science in my own field. There have been publications in various scientific journals and magazines.

Circumstances forced me and my family to flee from my native place because of barbaric acts of the militants in the valley, leaving me and my family as migrants. Up to 1990, we lived at Baghat, Barzulla, Srinagar, with a big chunk of land and a huge building, now raised to ground. The city had become familiar with firearms and weapons. Foreigners had cropped up everywhere, like unfamiliar trees and no one asked who sent them or why they came.

I have my wife Sarla with me. She is M.A. B Ed. and has worked in the Education Department. She has cooperated with me through thick and thin, and she bore me three beautiful children Sandeep, Sanjla and Sumeet. All of them have been given superior higher education at a time when the conditions in Kashmir were extremely bad. I along with my wife had to prove in harder times how to keep the crucial education of our children going. We Kashmiris have a belief, that, our wealth is to give highest education to our children. In difficult times our children co-operated with us. They perhaps put in extra hours of labor and got admissions in various professional colleges on their own steam. They have a strong educational background, married, and are happy where ever they are, living in exile.

Many of my community, the Kashmiri Pandits, a "Kashur Batta" left Kashmir. I became a migrant in my own country. Not one, not hundreds, not thousands, but in lakhs, Kashmiri Pandits were forced to leave Kashmir. All this happened in the year 1990, a bad year for us.

I along with my wife and children have widely travelled to various countries like United States of America, the United Kingdom, India, and Canada. Now we belong to all worlds, and all men are our brothers, and all women as our sisters.

Kashmir Shaivism can be summed up in one sentence: 'Everything is Chiti, everything is Consciousness'. All questions appear in Consciousness and nowhere else! Of Her own free will, Chiti unfolds the universe on Her own screen. Consciousness creates the universe of Her own free will. Consciousness is free and Shiva unfolds the universe within Himself. Consciousness is a big question.

In Kashmir we had a 14th Century poetess, Lal Ded (1320-1392). I love to memorize most of the wise sayings of Lal Ded.

My special thanks to Sumeet Misri, my son, for doing editing on computer including the styling.

Sham S. Misri

Redmond, Seattle, USA

Washington, USA

20th Jan.2013

Dr. M.L Babu

I was born and brought up in Kashmir. I lived in Kashmir till my migration from valley in 1990.Kashmiri pandits presently are scattered a lover world, thanks to militancy in valley. Kashmiri Pandit at present is at the verge of extinction after being uprooted from his home. Our children are fast loosing track of their great past but are also loosing cultural values too. The day is not for off when he would not know who he is and where from he came? Just to keep him aware of our rich heritage, an attempt has been made in this article to tell him about SHAIVISM which originated from our Mother Land and its relevance today.

My interests besides Medicine are in Ancient History of Kashmir, Vedas and Ancient India. I have travelled a lot, interacted with various people and perused various religious books. I have come to conclusion that India's past is hidden in Puranic stories. These stories are acting like cover of a fruit. Just like cover of a fruit hides a delicious fruit inside, in same way Puranic stories hide nectar of human wisdom inside.

I have written various articles , published book long back My professional articles stand published in both and international journals Now I will be concentrating on my passion, i.e. Puranic stories and their relevance today.

I am thankful to my sweet wife Kusum who has encouraged me to write and helped in proof reading. Special thanks to my daughters, Suprigya and Sucriti who provided me Laptop and technical assistance.

I thank Sandeep Misri, Julish Bhat and M.K.Bhan for their valuable suggestions and technical help.

Dr. M.L. Babu
Old Janipur Road, Jammu,
India.

About the Book

Kashmir Shaivism is a very vast subject. The matter is widely available free on internet. This may probably be so due to the fact that some missionaries and philanthropists want the religious matter to be available to the masses.

In order to have a much clear and lucid approach to the subject, the authors had aimed at making the same available in a capsule form easily to be understood and available to the people.

Besides this, there has been lot of criticism on the philosophy of Vedic religion [HIDUISM]- that this universe is Maya. It is being criticized on this ground, that this world is real as it produces phenomenon. But Vedanta clearly states that this world is illusion [MAYA]. This Maya is neither real nor unreal.

It was therefore, that to clarify the doubt - a project was under taken by the authors to compile, and consolidate the subject matter 'Kashmir Shaivism and Modern Science' in the form of a book.

Further, on the one hand the book gives a peep into the past philosophy of Kashmir Shaivism and on the other hand the author's try to clarify the doubt on scientific reasoning.

The authors feel that the book may prove helpful to the readers to understand the subject.

Essentially the book is an essence on Kashmir Shaivism and Modern Science.

The authors are thankful to the vast resource of study material and references that were available from various websites of the internet.

Bibliography, References and URLs

Greene Brian, *.Hidden Reality*

Kalla B. N, *Kashmir Saivism and its Echoes in Kashmiri Poetry,* Patrika

Kaw Dr. R. K, *Shaivism & Kashmir's Doctrine of 'Recognition' (Pratyabhijna)*

Koul M. L, *Guru in Kashmir Shaivism and Guru in Lalla Ded Vakh,* Kashmir Sentinel

Linda Johnson, *Philosophy and Spirituality,* Tantra and Teachings of Kashmir's Abhinavgupta, February 2004

Raina Dr. C. L, *Saivism in Prospect and Retrospect,*

Sadananda Dr K, *An Introduction to Vedanta.*

Swami Lakshman JOO, *Kashmir Shaivism: the secret supreme,* Sri Sat guru Publications,

1991. Kash. Shaivism Ref.

Swami Shankarananda, *the Yoga of Kashmir Shaivism: Consciousness is everything.*

Motilal Banarsidass Publishers, Publication Date: 2003

Benol Salazar, Metamusica, Musicosophia, Londrina, Instituto de Yoga and Musicoterapia, 1987, Chapter "The Ancient Science of Sound." translated from Spanish by Maria Alice Mendonca.

Parā-trīsikā Vivaraṇa, Jaideva Singh

The Triadic Heart of Siva, Paul Muller-Ortega

https://www.google.com/

https://www.google.com/

http://www.shaivism.net/lalded2/2.html

http://www.koausa.org/Glimpses/abhinava.html

http://www.koausa.org/Glimpses/Pratyabhijna.html

http://www.koausa.org/Patrika/saivism.html

http://www.koausa.org/Shaivism/article2.html

http://www.koausa.org/Saints/KrishnaJooRazdan/article2.html

http://www.koausa.org/KoshSam/Krishna_joo.html

http://www.koausa.org/Saints/LalDed/article2.html

http://www.koausa.org/Glimpses/Roopa_Bhawani.html

http://www.shaivism.net/articles/5.html

http://www.esamskriti.com/essay-chapters/Tantra-and-Teachings-of-Kashmir%60s-Abhinavgupta-1.aspx
http://ikashmir.net/govindkaul/index.html
http://www.scribd.com/doc/103660712/KASHMIR-SHAIVISM-Lakshman-Joo-Corrected-Version

---

http://www.scribd.com/doc/45305873/shaivism
http://www.shivayoga.org/html/kashmirshaivism1.html
http://en.wikipedia.org/wiki/Mahamandaleshwar_Swami_Shankarananda_%28Shiva_Yoga%29
http://en.wikipedia.org/wiki/Vedanta
http://en.wikipedia.org/wiki/Kapalika
http://en.wikipedia.org/wiki/Kashmir_Shaivism
http://www.kashmirshaivism.org/introduction.html
http://sivasakti.com/articles/tantra/introduction-to-tantra-art21.html
http://sivasakti.com/articles/woman/shakti-art26.html
http://sivasakti.com/articles/tantra/orgasm-art26.html
http://sivasakti.com/articles/tantra/shakti-art35.html
http://sivasakti.net/articles/tantra/shiva-shakti-art37.html
http://sivasakti.com/articles/man/shakti-art137.html
http://sivasakti.com/articles/man/shakti-art138.html
http://sivasakti.com/articles/man/shakti-art139.html
http://sivasakti.com/articles/man/shakti-art140.html
http://sivasakti.net/articles/couple/shakti-art44.html
http://sivasakti.com/articles/tantra/kashmiri-shaivism-art131.html
http://sivasakti.com/articles/tantra/kashmiri-shaivism-art132.html
http://sivasakti.com/articles/tantra/kashmiri-shaivism-art133.html
http://sivasakti.com/articles/tantra/kashmiri-shaivism-art134.html
http://sivasakti.com/articles/tantra/kashmiri-shaivism-art135.html
http://sivasakti.com/articles/tantra/kashmiri-shaivism-art136.html
http://sivasakti.com/articles/tantra/kashmiri-shaivism-art137.html
http://sivasakti.com/articles/tantra/kashmiri-shaivism-art138.html
http://sivasakti.com/articles/tantra/kashmiri-shaivism-art139.html
http://sivasakti.com/articles/tantra/kashmiri-shaivism-art140.html
http://sivasakti.com/articles/tantra/kashmiri-shaivism-art141.html
http://sivasakti.com/articles/tantra/kashmiri-shaivism-art142.html
http://sivasakti.com/articles/tantra/kashmiri-shaivism-art143.html
http://sivasakti.com/articles/tantra/kashmiri-shaivism-art144.html

http://sivasakti.com/articles/tantra/kashmiri-shaivism-art145.html
http://sivasakti.com/articles/tantra/kashmiri-shaivism-art146.html
http://sivasakti.com/articles/tantra/kashmiri-shaivism-art147.html
http://sivasakti.com/articles/tantra/kashmiri-shaivism-art148.html
http://sivasakti.com/articles/tantra/kashmiri-shaivism-art149.html
http://sivasakti.com/articles/tantra/kashmiri-shaivism-art150.html
http://sivasakti.com/articles/tantra/kashmiri-shaivism-art151.html
http://sivasakti.com/articles/tantra/kashmiri-shaivism-art152.html
http://shehjar.com/jlbhat/articles.html
http://www.shehjar.com/viewArticle.do?method=magazinearticleprinterfriendly&maga_arti_id=1148
https://ikashmir.net/mlkoul/pratybhijjna.html
http://wp.jeremysilman.com/spiritual_journey_ss/you_are_your_awareness.html
http://www.iep.utm.edu/kashmiri/
http://www.answers.com/topic/shaivism
http://www.answers.com/topic/hinduism
http://www.shaivism.net/articles/1.html
www.manta.com/Website_Submission
http://shivayoga.org/html/swamishankarananda.html
http://www.koausa.org/Shaivism/
http://www.siddhayoga.org/glossary
http://www.zoominfo.com/#!search/profile/person?personId=1386330747&targetid=profile
https://www.google.com/#hl=en&tbo=d&output=search&sclient=psy-ab&q=Guru+in+Kashmir+Shaivism+and+Guru+in+Lalla+Ded+Vakh+By+Prof.+M.L.+Koul+&oq=Guru+in+Kashmir+Shaivism+and+Guru+in+Lalla+Ded+Vakh+By+Prof.+M.L.+Koul&gs_l=hp.12...63770.63770.0.65938.1.1.0.0.0.0.106.106.0j1.1.0.les%3B..0.0....1c.dHVic5sTLAA&pbx=1&bav=on.2,or.r_gc.r_pw.r_cp.r_qf.&bvm=bv.41524429,d.cGE&fp=b31687ff2a7cb08a&biw=1525&bih=666
https://www.google.com/#hl=en&tbo=d&output=search&sclient=psy-ab&q=Kashmir+Shaivism+%28Ka%C5%9Bmir+%C5%9Aaivism%29+is+a+school+of+%C5%9Aaivism+consisting+of+Trika+and+its+philosophical+expression+Pratyabhij%C3%B1a.+It+is+categorized+by+various+scholars+as+monistic[2]+idealism+%28absolute+idealism%2C+theistic+monism%2C+realistic+idealism%2C+transcendental+physicalism+or+&oq=Kashmir+Shaivism+%28Ka%C5%9Bmir+%C5%9Aaivism%29+is+a+school+of+%C5%9Aaivism+consisting+of+Trika+and+its+philosophical+expression+Pratyabhij%C3%B1a.+It+is+categorized+by+various+scholars+as+monistic[2]+idealism+%28absolute+idealism%2C+theistic+monism%2C+realistic+idealism%2C+transcendental+physicalism+or+&gs_l=hp.12...407

146

1.4071.0.6470.1.1.0.0.0.0.0.0..0.0.les%3B..0.1...1c.EsF8DMIXUp0&pbx=1&bav=
on.2,or.r_gc.r_pw.r_cp.r_qf.&bvm=bv.41524429,d.cGE&fp=b31687ff2a7cb08a&b
iw=1525&bih=666
https://www.google.com/#hl=en&tbo=d&spell=1&q=Kashmir+Shaivism+By+Dr.+
Virendra+Qazi+Email:+lalleshwari+int_trust%40hotmail.com&sa=X&ei=71YBU
Z7pM4WeiQLR0YCoBw&sqi=2&ved=0CC8QvwUoAA&bav=on.2,or.r_gc.r_pw.
r_cp.r_qf.&bvm=bv.41524429,d.cGE&fp=b31687ff2a7cb08a&biw=1525&bih=66
6
https://www.google.com/#hl=en&tbo=d&output=search&sclient=psy-
ab&q=INTRODUCTION+TO+KASHMIRI+SHAIVISM+&oq=INTRODUCTION
+TO+KASHMIRI+SHAIVISM+&gs_l=hp.12..0i13i30.5806.5806.0.9487.1.1.0.0.0
.0.92.92.1.1.0.les%3B..0.0...1c.gQDCPZ13FRI&pbx=1&bav=on.2,or.r_gc.r_pw.r_
cp.r_qf.&bvm=bv.41524429,d.cGE&fp=b31687ff2a7cb08a&biw=1525&bih=666
https://www.google.com/#hl=en&tbo=d&sclient=psy-
ab&q=John+Hughes+is+a+disciple+of+Sw%C4%81m%C4%AB+Lak%E1%B9%
A3man-
j%C5%AB.&oq=John+Hughes+is+a+disciple+of+Sw%C4%81m%C4%AB+Lak%
E1%B9%A3man-
j%C5%AB.&gs_l=hp.12...3502.3502.0.5637.1.1.0.0.0.0.69.69.1.1.0.les%3B..0.0...1
c.9ADxno00M9k&pbx=1&bav=on.2,or.r_gc.r_pw.r_cp.r_qf.&bvm=bv.41524429,
d.cGE&fp=b31687ff2a7cb08a&biw=1525&bih=666
https://www.google.com/#hl=en&tbo=d&output=search&sclient=psy-
ab&q=++K+A+S+H+M+I+R+++S+H+A+I+V+I+S+M&oq=++K+A+S+H+M+I+
R+++S+H+A+I+V+I+S+M&gs_l=hp.12...5624.5624.0.8547.1.1.0.0.0.0.80.80.1.1.
0.les%3B..0.0...1c.2.N_9SjMX5bkQ&pbx=1&bav=on.2,or.r_gc.r_pw.r_cp.r_qf.&b
vm=bv.41524429,d.cGE&fp=b31687ff2a7cb08a&biw=1525&bih=666
https://www.google.com/#hl=en&tbo=d&output=search&sclient=psy-
ab&q=CHAPTER+8:+Lal+Vaakhs+-
+Their+Journey+from+Memory+to+Manuscript+&oq=CHAPTER+8:+Lal+Vaakh
s+-
+Their+Journey+from+Memory+to+Manuscript+&gs_l=hp.12...380017.380017.0.
382803.1.1.0.0.0.0.150.150.0j1.1.0.les%3B..0.0...1c.2.wC7hsPfvzKU&pbx=1&bav
=on.2,or.r_gc.r_pw.r_cp.r_qf.&bvm=bv.41524429,d.cGE&fp=b31687ff2a7cb08a&
biw=1525&bih=666
https://www.google.com/#hl=en&sugexp=les%3B&gs_rn=1&gs_ri=hp&tok=AShf
HKjUa69G3MuRN9YrXQ&cp=28&gs_id=9l&xhr=t&q=Science+and+Kashmir+S
haivism&es_nrs=true&pf=p&tbo=d&output=search&sclient=psy-
ab&oq=Science+and+Kashmir+Shaivism&gs_l=&pbx=1&bav=on.2,or.r_gc.r_pw.r

_cp.r_qf.&bvhttp://www.koausa.org/Saints/LalDed/article2.htmlm=bv.41524429,d.cGE&fp=b31687ff2a7cb08a&biw=1525&bih=666

Other Books by the Same Author(s)

1. Lal Ded Of Kashmir Saint Poetess: A Catalogue of Lal Vakhs
2. Kashmir - A Concise History: Mahabharata Epoch 3067 BCE to Modi Era 2016 A.D
3. The Aryan Invasion Theory - A Subterfuge: A Scientific Look
4. Tibet: Earthly Paradise
5. Kali Maa: The Dawn of Woman and Beyond
6. Maa Ganga: Mythology, Mystery and Science
7. Shiv and Shakti: A Journey of Life
8. The Ten Departures of Kashmiri Pandits
9. Tales from Kashmir, Part-1
10. Tales from Kashmir, Part-2
11. Tales from Kashmir, Part-3
12. Tales from Kashmir, Part-4
13. Tales from Kashmir, Part-5
14. The Wandering Pandit
15. Wonderful Stories for Children, Book-1
16. A Peep Into America's Past
17. Silkworm Breeding Made Easy
18. Collected Poems of Pt. Krishen Joo Razdan, By J. N. Misri, Vol. 1, 2,3,4,5 and 6[Edited and Published]
19. Travels Through America And Canada
20. When I Met Her
21. The Ultimate Fishing Rod
22. Kashmir: The Book of Anecdotes
23. Tour to 5 Countries in Europe
24. Cleopatra-Harmachis-Part-1-Love-Lord
25. Cleopatra and Harmachis - Part-2: The Finding of Treasure
26. Amorous Ancient Mythological Tales
27. The Sleeping Eyes

Made in the USA
Middletown, DE
28 February 2019